T0368426

A SEEKER'S JOURNEY

A MEMOIR OF MUSINGS AND MEANING

FRAN BERKELL-RAFFERTY

Balboa Press books may be ordered through booksellers or by contacting:

Balboa Press
A Division of Hay House
1663 Liberty Drive
Bloomington, IN 47403
www.balboapress.com
844-682-1282

Interior Image Credit: Fran Berkell-Rafferty

ISBN: 979-8-7652-4808-9 (sc)
ISBN: 979-8-7652-4809-6 (hc)
ISBN: 979-8-7652-4807-2 (e)

Library of Congress Control Number: 2023923727

Print information available on the last page.

Balboa Press rev. date: 06/05/2024

BALBOA.PRESS
A DIVISION OF HAY HOUSE

To the memory of my mother, Doris Berkell, who by her example taught me all I needed to know about kindness, compassion, generosity, and unconditional love.

Foreword

I nspired by the backdrop and magnificence of the majestic Blue Ridge Mountains, *A Seeker's Journey: A Memoir of Musings and Meaning,* by Fran Berkell-Rafferty, is a story for all seasons of a person's life; for youth who need guidance on how to think about what it means to be; for the young adult and those in midlife who have not yet been touched by illness and adversity as a gentle reminder to value and protect the beautiful bodies that are vessels that house their souls; and to those in later life as a message of faith and courage to hold on to one's faith and live according to your values, no matter the challenges that lie ahead.

With raw emotion, authenticity, and vulnerability, Fran shares her heart as she faces her fears and challenges of living with scleroderma and later a seizure disorder post a hemorrhagic stroke. She invites the reader in and unabashedly allows you to get to know her as she openly faces her loss and grief during her poststroke rehabilitation.

Fran is an inspiration to us all. When presented with the opportunity to change what she can, Fran invites us to cheer for her dogged determination to remain undefeated, and at the same time, cry alongside her even retroactively when her wisdom and inner knowing informs her to surrender to what is.

With a gift for the ability to think and write metaphorically, Fran reveals her humility and a deep sense of connectedness to all of nature and all living things. Her wonder at the mystical, magical nature of our planet inspires her musings about life and how nature mirrors the changes, twists, and turns of her own life. While reading, it is easy to find oneself reflecting on one's own mystical experiences and life purpose within the planet. Set in the lushness of the Appalachian Trail, one is inspired to take a trip there, see the beauty of this wondrous setting, and allow oneself to experience this vortex of healing.

Through her childhood experiences of having felt loved and fully accepted, Fran informs us how to parent and how to nurture the souls of the next generation. Her footprints are a road map for a better future if we will only listen and allow. Fran is a champion at living and loving. Her life's journey is a protocol for patience, gratitude, loving-kindness, and compassion. Through her healing journey, Fran's writing is an example of how to live fearlessly, courageously, fully present, awake, aware, and with fortitude and resilience.

Easy to connect with and easy to love, Fran Berkell-Rafferty invites you to know her. She is deeply curious and compassionate and wants to know you. Being with her, you find her asking you questions because of her deep caring desire to know you and be close. You find Fran listening intently with interest and more questions that follow, and you feel drawn to answer, to connect with her, and to love her openness and empathy.

From early in her life, Fran's wisdom, self-knowledge, and deep understanding of the world around her reveal a person who lives a values-based life. Throughout her health struggles, she fights to hold onto her values of faith that God's plan is for the good and that the "being-angels" that come through her life are divinely sent to sustain and support her unstoppable drive toward healing. Her unshakable faith in God's love and unwavering belief that if you point your compass in the direction of God's light, good things will come, underscore her willingness to live fully in the face of her challenges, open to whatever life brings with acceptance and growth. Holding onto and living a values-based life, Fran faces her truths honestly and commits to walking the talk, to living her proclaimed values for better or for worse.

A Seeker's Journey: A Memoir of Musings and Meaning is a must-read for all generations. Those who grew up in the social-historical times of Fran's youth will laugh at her memoirs of our teenage follies. Young adults today often live in a virtual land of isolation and alienation on the brink of nowhere to connect and feel fragile and easily broken. Hopefully, they will have their longings to love and be loved piqued by Fran's warmth and gentle kindness enough to begin to step outward and begin to look inward. Her steadfast drive, motivation, and zest for life, and her gratitude and eagerness to give back and pay it forward are examples to us all of how to live fearlessly, courageously, purposefully, and fully present.

Thank you, Fran, for your love, friendship, and most important, for your inspiration on how to live and love.

Robin A. Avery, PhD
Licensed Psychologist

Acknowledgments

I would like to thank the special people who have played vital roles in my journey thus far and those who have helped me bring this creative project to fruition.

To my dear friends Ivonne and Chris Cintron-Pecoraro, who encouraged me to put my compilation of writings into book form and spent countless hours helping me do that; to my dear, lifelong childhood friend Betsy Hofstadter, who took the time to read through my initial manuscript and provide invaluable feedback; to my sister, Susan Loewenstein, who has been a best friend and confidante as we have shared so many of our life journeys by each other's side, a special thank you to both her and her husband, David Loewenstein, whose love, support, and guidance helped me navigate my way through many of life's challenges, especially my most recent health issues; to my father, Gerald Berkell, for his unconditional love, kind and gentle words, and offerings of wisdom, and for always believing in me and encouraging me to pursue my dreams; to my children, Jennifer, Michael, and Kyle, who provided me with much-needed technical support at various stages of the publication and editing process, and who inspire me every day to be a better human; to my husband, Kevin, who has always encouraged me to share my writings with the outside world and who has stood by me and offered his unwavering love and support for the past five decades; to Dr. Robin Avery, who was interested in reading what I had written and whose feedback provided the final impetus I needed to take the leap of faith and submit my manuscript for publication; and, of course, a very special thank you to my mom, Doris Berkell, to whom this book is dedicated, and although she passed away prior to the book's publication, it was by her example that I learned everything I needed to know about kindness, compassion, generosity, and unconditional love.

Thank you to all of them and to the countless other friends, family members, teachers, colleagues, and individuals whose paths have crossed with mine over the past six decades on this exciting and often challenging journey.

Contents

Introduction

If only I may grow: firmer, simpler, quieter, warmer.

—Dag Hammarskjold.

first remember seeing that quote on a small poster during my first year of college. It was the mid-1970s, and the nation was just coming out of some very turbulent times.

The previous summer, our country witnessed the unprecedented resignation of a sitting president, and that historical event had been preceded by a decade fueled by violence, chaos, and calls for radical change. Yes, a decade in which we mourned the deaths of three of our most influential leaders—John F. Kennedy, Martin Luther King Jr., and Robert Kennedy—whose young lives had been cut short by bullets from an assassin's gun. A decade when sit-ins and marches became ordinary events as people rose to protest an unpopular war and to demand civil rights and voting rights for all. A decade when the words *antiestablishment, love-ins,* and *Woodstock* helped to define a generation.

I was in my preteen and early teenage years during most of that turbulent decade, not quite old enough to participate in the sit-ins and marches or attend Woodstock. But now, here I was, in the fall of 1974, beginning my post-high school educational studies and living away from home for the first time in my young life. I was on the precipice of becoming an adult and found myself asking new questions and exploring new ideas. And it was at this transitional time I came upon that poster with the Dag Hammarskjold quotation. I must admit, that although I do not remember exactly where I was when I first saw it, I remember quite vividly how those nine simple words resonated with me. I somehow knew at that moment that there was something special in that message, so I bought a copy of the poster and hung it in my dorm room. I am not sure what happened to that small paper poster. I guess it got lost or tossed at some point in one of my several moves to new living quarters during those college years. But the message on that poster, the significance of those nine words, never left me. And for the past forty years, the simple message in that quotation has served as a kind of mantra, a guiding force in my life.

Throughout these last four decades, while busy pursuing undergraduate and postgraduate education, getting married, working full time, and giving birth to and raising three wonderful children, I would often find myself pausing and questioning whether I was indeed growing in the direction of that mantra. During all the hustle and bustle, trials and tribulations of everyday life, had I succeeded in, or was I succeeding in, achieving such an aspiration? I guess the simple answer is that while I am not completely there yet, and perhaps never will be, I believe I have made considerable strides and will continue in my efforts to become that person.

The words, the writings in this book, reflect my journey seeking to grow firmer, simpler, quieter, warmer.

As I delved into this project of sifting through the writings I have composed over the past several decades to put many of them together in actual book form, a bound format that could be shared with the outside world, I noticed some common themes running throughout many of the pieces. I decided it would make sense to choose a few themes or categories and arrange the writings accordingly. After much deliberation, I chose nature, human connections, spirituality and the divine, virtues, transitions, and life lessons.

The questions I asked, the answers I sought, the thoughts that I pondered that were at the center of my writings, so often at its essence, contained undertones of several, if not all, of those respective categories. Each of these themes seemed so intimately connected, so deeply intertwined. Nature by its very existence teaches us so many life lessons, connects us so deeply to the divine and our spirituality, offers us insights into our human connections. Life lessons, what we learn from all that we encounter in this world, are so dependent on the transitions we go through, the virtues we value and exemplify, the human connections we make, and the spiritual paths we choose to follow.

And so, while I have done my best to place each writing in the section where I feel it most belongs, I recognize that, just like us humans, the subjects of these writings rarely fit neatly into any one box. They do not exist in a vacuum. They are often complex, interconnected parts of the larger whole.

Ultimately, the words, the writings in this book, reflect my earnest seeking. I hope you will join me on my journey to grow firmer, simpler, quieter, warmer.

NATURE

Nature has been a source of peace and inspiration for me for as long as I can remember. I recall as a young child being fascinated by the tiny snails creeping slowly up and down the walls and sidewalks outside our South Florida home, amazed at their ability to cling so firmly to the surface via the rubbery bodies within their multicolored shells. During my childhood, I spent hours at the neighborhood park, eagerly looking at the ground in the hope of witnessing a rabbit or crab peer out of one of their homes, a perfectly rounded dirt hole. And I would often venture over to the lake to scoop up tadpoles swimming feverishly about in the shallow waters. Sometimes I placed the tadpoles in a jar filled with lake water, took them home, and watched in awe as their limbs grew and their bodies developed. Then I'd release them back into their natural habitat as fully formed frogs.

Growing up in South Florida, I learned to have a great appreciation for a wide variety of tropical trees and plants and, of course, the ocean. I spent a great deal of time at the beach, basking in the sun (before knowing about the importance of applying sunscreen for protection) and frolicking in the salt water. I was in awe of the vastness of the ocean and learned at a young age to be respectful of the magnitude of her changing tides. The calm, flat surface could sometimes hide the dangers presented by the fierce currents of the riptide lurking below. I experienced on more than one occasion the enormous strength and power of such tides.

During my teenage years, I had the opportunity to attend summer camp in the Blue Ridge Mountains of North Carolina. It was there that I was first exposed to a terrain and climate quite different from the South Florida tropics I was used to. I fell in love with the beauty of the lush mountain range, the freshwater streams, and the cool summer nights. I appreciated the many types of animals and foliage living in this new environment.

In the years that followed, I was able to return to the Blue Ridge Mountains several times as a camper, a college student, a young married woman, and a new mom. Over those same years, I also had the opportunity to travel to many other places throughout this country and even to a few other parts of the world. But there was always something so special to me about those North Carolina mountains. They just seemed to reach out and draw me in.

In the fall of 1989, I was pregnant with the second of my three children when my father bought a lot and built a home in that mountain area I had first fallen in love with over two decades prior. For the past twenty-nine years, my husband and I and our children have had the good fortune of spending many holidays and family gatherings in that home amid the beauty of that mountain terrain.

In the summer of 2015, I traveled to the North Carolina house to spend what was supposed to be a couple of weeks with my dad, who was there for the summer. When I left South Florida, there was some work being done at our house. The plan was that my husband would complete the work at home and then come up to North Carolina, and we would drive back to South Florida together. The scope of the work ended up being more involved than originally expected, so my two-week visit was extended to eight.

Those additional unexpected six weeks turned into something quite transformative. I found myself with a lot of unscheduled, quiet time alone. In addition to my usual morning runs, I would go almost every day for a late afternoon walk on the mountain trails. During those walks, I began to feel more deeply connected to my natural surroundings than I normally did. While I am usually cognizant of the beauty around me and appreciative of the special gifts Mother Nature so frequently offers, this felt different. There was a profound intensity enveloping me. It was as though the trees, the animals, the sights, and the sounds were more alive than usual. They seemed to be speaking to me in loud and clear tones, triggering my creative juices, urging me to express these feelings, to put pen to paper. And that is what I did. Most of the writings I have included in this section titled "Nature" were written during my bonus six-week period.

The Butterfly

Sitting outside on the deck this morning, surrounded by the backdrop of these Carolina mountains, my attention is drawn to a beautiful golden butterfly circling about. I find myself gazing in awe as this tiny creature flutters so gracefully amid the blades of green grass. I watch as it pauses briefly to rest upon and seek nourishment from a nearby flower bed. As I walk toward it to observe it more closely, I am amazed at the symmetry of this delicate life force, the identical patterns that comprise its four wings, and the power that these paper-thin propellers possess. My attempts to capture this elusive insect as it floats by prove to be an exercise in futility as it weaves effortlessly through the air, remaining just beyond grasp, merely teasing me into thinking that it can be caught or that it is about to land on my willing shoulder.

As I continue focusing on this tiny creature, I find myself pondering over the short life span of these fragile beings and the remarkable transformations made in their brief stay. From the creeping, crawling caterpillar to the immobile, dormant, protective web of the cocoon to the beautiful, soaring object shedding its light upon the landscape, so very many changes in such a limited amount of time. Is this not similar to the patterns of our lives here on this earthly plane?

From our physical alterations to our intellectual growth to our emotional shifts and spiritual evolution, do we humans not undergo an amazing number of transitions in a relatively limited time, continually transforming as we navigate our ways through the trials and tribulations encountered in this earth school? In what often seems like a blink of an eye, we go from newborn to toddler to young child to adolescent to adult to middle-aged to senior. Isn't our existence in our physical bodies nothing more than a fleeting moment in the grand scheme of the universe? Are not each of us just tiny pixels in the big picture, mere grains of sand on the wide-open beach, small waves rolling among the tides of the vast ocean? Is not our time here merely a temporary layover on a larger journey?

We need to recognize that the world we inhabit is continually shifting, and we, as forces of nature within it, are ever changing. Perhaps, like the butterfly, our destiny here is to evolve into magnificent beings, to shed a bit more grace and beauty upon this land during our brief stay, and ultimately, to spread our wings and soar.

Nature's Lessons

We still do not know one thousandth of one percent of what nature has revealed to us.

—Albert Einstein

There is so much we humans can learn from observing the natural world around us. If we take the time to tune into our surroundings, quiet our minds, really listen, open our eyes and truly see, we can sense the parallels between the ebb and flow of our lives and the cycles, the patterns, throughout nature's landscape.

Just as the sky can change from dark gray and cloudy to bright blue and sunny, and the winds can shift from strong gusts to a gentle breeze, so, too, do we find our thoughts, our moods, our entire outlooks transitioning from foggy and confused to clearheaded and certain, from melancholy and pensive to upbeat and joyful. Sometimes these shifts are triggered by specific events. Other times, they seem to occur for no apparent reason. Regardless of whether or not we can pinpoint the cause, we must accept that it is all equally important, necessary parts of the journey. Just as the seasons come and go—the cold, bare days of winter give way to the warm, budding fullness of spring, and the bright vibrant greens of summer become the gold, red, and orange leaves of fall—so, too, do our lives revolve around both subtle and intense transformations.

As is true in nature, our lives move in a certain rhythmic flow, and we need to pay attention to this rhythm. We must recognize the peaceful essence that is at its core. We need to remember in times of darkness that light is waiting to break through. Trust that behind the gray clouds and falling raindrops sits a colorful rainbow and clear skies. Believe that beneath the rocky surface of the turbulent waters lies a calm, easy stillness. Know that a vast placid ocean rests just beyond the fierce whitecapped waves rushing to the shore. We are creatures of a dimension characterized by duality. We seem to have sharper perceptions when we recognize that we need dark to see light and vice versa.

Through it all—the highs, the lows, the tumult, the calm, the clarity, the confusion—we must keep in mind what nature seems to inherently know so well: It is all part of the grand design, integral to maintaining the necessary balance, vital to the overall growth process. So many of us give in to the impulses to fight against it, ignore it, resist, or try to force it away. Rather, I am learning to surrender to it, allow myself to drift amid the currents, willing to ride out the storms along the way.

At the same time, we must not view ourselves as passive observers, helpless travelers who should give up or succumb to the numerous obstacles encountered on our paths. Instead, we need to remain active, invested participants, steadfast in our attempts to keep pushing forward, moving ever closer toward the light.

As we continue our steady uphill climb, we need to take time to pause and become still, so we may reflect on and truly soak in and appreciate the incredible similarities between the patterns of our lives and the multiple patterns in the natural environment. As we pay attention to the many fine-tuned details, as we attempt to absorb the comparisons between the two, we realize the brilliance of Mother Nature, the breadth and depth of her knowledge. What a masterful instructor she truly is. I thank this wonderful teacher for providing us with the opportunity to partake in this learning experience, for opening her classroom to us, and for sharing this fascinating curriculum. For exposing us to and helping to teach us some of the greatest material ever taught. For allowing us to enroll and partake in this unique and awe-inspiring course titled "Nature's Lessons."

Nature's Song

I am taking a late-afternoon walk along a wooded path in the Carolina mountains, enjoying the feeling of the rugged terrain beneath my feet on this bright, relatively cool summer day. I have decided to quiet my mind, to not speak a word. I am determined to listen, really listen, to all the magnificent sounds filtering through these beautiful surroundings. No cell phones, no headphones, no radios or human voices. Nothing to distract from my ability to hear all the wondrous melodies circling.

Focusing in on every minute detail, on the unique vibration accompanying each note. The chirping of the birds, the rustling of the leaves, the soft howl of the winds, the swooshing of the spring waters, and the squishing of the pebbles and rocks below my sneakers. The scurrying of the chipmunk as it flees into the dense brush, the scattering of the skunk as it moves quickly off the path. The squeaking of the mouse as it hurries along, attempting to stay clear of the many predators roaming nearby. Even the hush of the deer as it suddenly stops in its tracks on hearing what it perceives to be the potentially threatening sound of human footsteps.

As I continue walking quietly, listening intently, I realize that I am amid a wonderful performance. I am attending a magnificent concert featuring some of nature's finest. A perfect harmony of so many melodious blends, all coming together as one very beautiful, breathtaking, awe-inspiring symphony. Once again, Mother Nature, in all her glory, sheds her light and beauty upon the land.

As I continue my quiet walk along the wooded path of these Carolina mountains, I pause to look up at the crystal blue sky and the golden, yellow sun shining so brightly. I marvel at the radiant beams of light flickering down through the trees and the vibrant green leaves swaying gently in the breeze. In that moment, it dawns on me that this is just another ordinary day amid nature's bounty. I realize that God has again provided me with the special opportunity to partake in one of the divine's most spectacular events. In my silence, I have been able to hear what might be the greatest musical composition I have ever heard, the only truly original "Nature's Song."

Picture-Perfect Day

The trees are now mostly bare. The golden-yellow and bright red leaves that enveloped them just days before are now scattered along the ground. The sky is a misty gray, quite a change from the crystal blue that it had been throughout most of the previous week. Rain is falling steadily, its drops slowly saturating the soil that had been quite dry and firm. The winds have calmed, settling down from the howling of their strong gusts last night but still more potent than the gentle sway that caressed the landscape a few days ago.

All of it is so very beautiful. All a reflection of the many faces of Mother Nature. Her subtleties and her intense roars. Her quiet presence and her more tumultuous side. Her calms and her storms. Her light and her darkness. Each is an important and necessary part of the whole. Each a representation of the twists and turns, the ever-changing patterns of the natural world.

There is so much we humans can learn from this wonderful teacher. If we pay attention to her every move, if we tune in and listen to her many sounds, if we look at and truly see her wondrous sights, we will recognize the many parallels between her shifts and the ebb and flow within our lives. We will perhaps better understand our places within this vast environment and realize that we are a part of something so much greater than ourselves. This insight, this perspective, will hopefully enable us to feel more deeply connected to all living things with which and with whom we share this planet, deepening our sensitivity to—and concern about—the sanctity of this earth and the need for us humans to protect it. Through our quiet, silent observations of Mother Nature, we can perhaps grow to be more compassionate, kinder, gentler, wiser beings.

As we pause along the way to soak in and appreciate the beauty and wonder of it all, we will realize that whether blue skies or gray, wind gusts or gentle breezes, sunshine or rain, it is all, at its essence, just as it is designed to be, an extraordinary picture-perfect day.

Sanctuary

Stepping out of the busyness, stopping our endless pursuit of getting somewhere else, is perhaps the most beautiful offering we can make to our spirit.

—Tara Brach

*S*anctuary. Defined in the *Merriam-Webster Dictionary* as "a holy or sacred place; the most sacred part of a place of worship; a building or room for religious worship; a place that provides shelter or protection."

There are several definitions for this word, but all seem to revolve around the common themes of a place of protection and sacredness.

As I continue moving forward on my journey, I find myself pondering over this word and its relevance in my life. I have come to realize that for me, it is within the natural world that I find my refuge, my haven. It is there, an environment filled with so much beauty and wonder, that I sense an aura of holiness that transcends time and space.

Taking the time to soak in, to attempt to absorb fully the many sights and sounds permeating every facet of nature's finest, I am reminded of the importance of all God's creations with which and with whom we share this planet. Listening to, and truly hearing the sweet chirping of the birds as they glide through the air, the gushing of stream waters after a heavy rainfall, the rustling of the leaves being caressed by gentle winds. Watching—and really seeing—the agility of the white-tailed deer running gracefully along the wooded path, the bright golden sun shining down from the crystal blue sky, the vibrant green grasses swaying back and forth in the soft breeze.

It is in such moments, when the mind is quiet and fully tuned into this melodious harmony echoing all around me, that I am reminded of the perfect balance at the center of this grand design. It is during these times that I can reflect on the similarities between nature's ebb and flow and the ups and downs, the periods of reaping and sowing in our lives. How the turbulent thunderstorm, with its heavy rains, thrashing winds, and booming roar, is followed by clear skies, stillness, and a near-dead silence. How the cold bareness of winter turns into the warm budding blossoms of spring. How the soil, dirt dry from recent drought, is suddenly drenched from floodwaters.

It is amid the backdrop of this resilient landscape that I can reflect on my life experiences thus far—the highs, the lows, the rocky, the smooth—and trust that it is all a necessary part of the overall growth process. That, just as nature does so beautifully, I have managed to, and will continue to persevere, survive, and grow stronger.

At the same time, it is in the serenity of these natural surroundings that I can focus on the present, turn my attention to and become fully engaged in the here and now, connect with the core of my being, and feel most deeply the presence of the divine Creator. It is here that I am at once humbled, awestruck, and inspired by the sanctity of it all. Overcome with a profound clarity and joy, an overwhelming peace and calm, knowing that I, and everything around me, have been touched by God's grace. These precious intervals of time are when I see so clearly the sacred in the ordinary, when I become intensely aware that my overflowing heart is filled with unimaginable gratitude for all the abundance in my life.

Indeed, it is in the refuge of Mother Nature that I find my shelter from the storm, that holy space where I can enjoy a reprieve from the stressful demands of daily life, a retreat from the superficial distractions and craziness of the material world. It is where I feel most protected, peaceful, and secure. Nature's wonderland is my very own private sanctuary.

Solitude

S olitude: quiet time alone. Not lonely, just alone, by oneself, in stillness. A time to step back, break away from the hustle, bustle, and numerous distractions of everyday life, and tune into that special place within. A time to allow our thoughts to wander, drift, and ponder the deeper, more profound questions about this world and the trajectory of our lives within it.

It is during such solitary intervals that we can reflect on our experiences thus far, the ups and downs, the highs and lows, the joys and sorrows. Time to evaluate what we have learned, what lessons we have been taught, what wisdom we have gained. Recognize in these reflective moments that life is a marathon, not a sprint, and that as we have done thus far, we must continue to persevere through the twists and turns and rough and rocky patches encountered along the way.

I have come to believe that solitude is vital to our well-being and overall growth process. It provides us with the opportunity to connect with the deepest, truest parts of ourselves, the cores of who we are and who we desire to be.

We need to take the time to withdraw from the rapid pace of our present-day instant gratification, technologically fueled society; seek a hiatus from the media, the infomercials, the commotion, the senseless, useless noise and chatter that consumes so much of our day-to-day existence. We must retreat to where we can rest our weary minds, step away from the chaos, turn down the volume, and in calm reflection, collect our thoughts, refuel our spirits, and reevaluate our priorities.

For me, it is the natural world that provides this space, that special place most conducive to being able to separate from the stresses and commitments of everyday life, recharge my batteries, and reconnect with my heart's call. It is there, immersed in the landscape of Mother Nature, detached from the concrete jungle and whirlwind of the man-made environment that I can tap into a sense of knowing, a certain clarity about the essence of it all. It is where I can look and really see, listen, and truly hear all the magnificent sights and sounds permeating throughout. I can fully appreciate, soak in, and absorb all the gifts, the abundance our Creator has bestowed on us. It is where I feel most deeply connected to all that is and feel so completely the amazing gift of God's grace. The quiet moments amid the sacred space of my natural surroundings are when I am reminded how crucial this solitary time is. It is as important to my soul as breathing is to my body.

It dawns on me how ironic it is that we can be among the masses, eating in a jam-packed restaurant, walking along a city street filled wall to wall with other people, attending a social event with a lot of hoopla and grandeur, and yet feel very much alone, lonely, lost in the crowd, not a part of but rather apart from. To the contrary. We can be alone in the silence of solitude, apart from the crowds, withdrawn, isolated from the masses, and yet feel so very connected, so much a part of, as though we have found our way and arrived safely home.

The Sun

The sun. That large star at the center of our solar system. The brightest object in the sky. Recognized throughout history by some cultures as a deity, the sun supports almost all life on earth and is the guiding force behind so much of this planet's climate and weather. Without the sun, we humans and all the natural resources that surround us would fail to survive.

These days I find myself looking at the sun with a profound sense of reverence and grace. I am in awe of her power, her beauty, and the strength of the beams of light that radiate so magnificently from her. Turning my face toward the sun, her warmth envelops me, allowing a certain calm and tranquility to flow through as her strong rays melt away any tensions trapped within.

I pause throughout the day to gaze at her, to appreciate the ever-changing majestic scenes that are created by her presence. From flickering through trees to shimmering upon mountaintops. From glimmering ice crystals on snow-covered fields to glistening whitecaps on the ocean's waves. From the clarity with which she appears amid crystal blue skies to her near invisibility when surrounded by white and gray clouds.

From dawn to dusk, sunrise to sunset, she is there, shedding her light upon the land, adding such an extraordinary essence to what otherwise might seem to be mere average occurrences of an ordinary day. I do so marvel at her glory, and I am so grateful for how she lights up my life and the lives of all living things on this planet we call Earth.

Trees

For many years now, I have found myself drawn to this natural resource. I am both mesmerized by the beauty of trees and inspired by the vital role they play in our ecosystem.

Throughout history, from ancient times to today, trees have held a significant place within both the physical and spiritual realms. In the physical world, they provide habitat and food for birds, other animals, and many insects. And they are perhaps most revered for their life-giving function of absorbing carbon dioxide from the air and releasing oxygen out into the atmosphere. Without the release of this oxygen, humans and other living organisms would fail to survive. Life on this earth would not be possible.

In the spiritual world, trees are regarded as a symbol of sacredness in many cultures. "The tree of life" and "the tree of knowledge of good and evil" are at the forefront of the Bible and the very foundation of the Judeo-Christian religions. In Buddhism, it is said that it is under the bodhi tree that Buddha sat and meditated and reached enlightenment. Pagans and Druids practiced worship among sacred groves of trees, and such groves are cherished as sacred natural sites by many modern-day societies. Indeed, the frequent association of trees with the concepts of life, wisdom, and knowledge makes this resource unique.

I often find myself marveling at the similarities between the physical structure of trees, the metamorphoses that they undergo, and our human tendencies and life patterns. The tree's roots anchor it to the soil, keeping it firmly attached to the ground while absorbing and storing food and nutrients necessary for its survival and growth. Our roots keep us grounded and provide us with the security and confidence to thrive. The trunk of the tree, like the torso of our bodies, provides the foundation upon which the tree can remain upright, allowing it to stand steady and strong while providing the base upon which its limbs can attach and grow. The limbs of the tree, its branches, serve as armrests where flowers can bloom, fruit can blossom, birds and other animals can rest, and leaves can bud. And it is the leaves, regarded as the food factories of the tree, that through the process of photosynthesis, use the energy from the sun to convert carbon dioxide from the atmosphere and water from the soil into sugar and oxygen. It is also the leaves that undergo the most visible transformation. As the seasons change, as summer gives way to cooler temperatures and the fewer numbers of daylight hours of fall, the leaves on many types of trees transform from their chlorophyll-filled shades of green to golden hues of red, orange, and yellow. The tree seems to inherently know that winter is on its way, and its leaves are preparing to shed as a strategy to survive the harsh cold weather that is on the horizon. As the leaves are shed and fall turns to winter, the tree is left bare, its limbs exposed. It waits patiently, seeming to endure without complaint, knowing that spring will soon arrive and with her will come new life.

Buds will reappear, flowers and fruit will bloom and blossom, birds will sing and nestle, and leaves will emerge as bright chlorophyll-filled green once again. And as spring turns to summer, the tree, having come full circle, is bursting with life, filled with a dense canopy of leaves providing shade from the blazing sun and branches offering safe harbor to birds and flowers and fruit. The tree basks in this remarkable period of renewal and growth, knowing that before long, the frigid weather will return, and to survive, it will need to bare itself once more.

Throughout the changes from full foliage to bare branches, from colorful to dull, from overflowing with life to stillness, the tree remains steady and resilient, its roots planted firmly in the ground, its trunk standing upright and strong. Its branches outstretched, open to receiving the life forms that need to rest and grow upon them. Is this not similar to the ebb and flow of our lives? While our life cycles may not revolve around exact seasonal patterns as that of trees, while we may not be able to predict with the same certainty when various changes in the seasons of our lives will occur, is it not worthy of comparison nonetheless? Like the trees, we experience periods when our lives feel full, abundant, vibrant, overflowing with growth and newness, when we seem to be reaping the benefits from seeds previously sown. And then, like the trees, there are times when our lives appear depleted, lacking, empty, bare, void of new growth and possibility, unable to reap or to sow. Like the trees, we must accept and quietly surrender to the varying conditions that we encounter. We must soak in and fully appreciate the favorable, colorful times. And perhaps most important, we must remember during the harsher adverse times to rely on the sturdy and resilient core of our foundations. We must delve deep into the roots that have been firmly planted within us, and with an open heart, know that this too shall pass. And that as is true in the life cycle of the tree, the bareness of the winter season will once again give way to the overflowing fullness and abundance of spring.

HUMAN CONNECTIONS

The world is a complex place, and I have certainly witnessed a lot of changes in my six decades within it. Nowhere are the changes more evident than in the area of technology, which in my lifetime, has advanced in unimaginable ways.

I remember attending the World's Fair in New York City in the summer of 1964, a few months before my eighth birthday. I was particularly awestruck by what I saw displayed in the General Motors Futurama Exhibit and the Bell Telephone Pavilion. Futurama provided a look into "The World of Tomorrow," aiming to take us everywhere that people of tomorrow would go, from outer space to the depths of the ocean. It provided us with glimpses into what cities of the future would look like and how new modes of transportation would take us to and from work and fly us to the moon. We were even given a tour of what the kitchen in our future homes might look like, including being equipped with a type of oven that could not only cook a roast in minutes but also have the potatoes to accompany it baked and ready to eat in less time than it would take to carve the roast. And then there was the refrigerated cart, which could be wheeled in to provide cold snacks and beverages to guests and family members in any room in the house. Today, the microwave oven is a standard feature in almost any home in this country, and the refrigerated cart is hardly considered a novel appliance.

While I was fascinated by so much of what I heard and saw in the Futurama exhibit, it was the Picturephone in the Bell Telephone Pavilion that I found most intriguing. To this day, over fifty years later, I can still conjure that image in my mind the first time I saw this incredible display of someone talking on the phone and being able to see the person he or she was talking to on a small video screen. At the time, and for many years that followed, I could not imagine being able to use the telephone in this manner. When I was a teenager in the late 1960s and early 1970s, my friends and I would spend hours on the phone. In those days, landlines were the only option; cordless phones did not exist. Caller identification, call waiting, hands-free, and voice mail were not yet available. When on the phone, you were stuck in one spot with the receiver held to your ear. The most you could do was invest in a longer phone cord, which would allow you to extend your distance a bit. If you needed to make a call when you were out and about, whether it be to check in with your parents or otherwise, you would locate the nearest pay phone booth, which could be found in most public facilities and on many street corners, and for ten or twenty cents, place the local call.

Looking back now, it is easy to understand why I was so intrigued by that display of the 1964 Picturephone. To me, it represented a revolutionary way of connecting with others. It provided an ability to see the person we were speaking to, a way of witnessing expressions, smiles, tears, and a way to be more in tune with their emotions and what the other person seemed to be feeling.

We have certainly come a long way from the technology of that Picturephone to the technological advances evidenced by the communication apparatuses of today. With the advent of the cell phone, we no longer need to sit in one place with a receiver held to our ear attached to a cord or search for a pay phone. Caller identification allows us to see who is trying to contact us, allowing us to choose to answer the call or send it to the prerecorded message in our voice-mail inbox. Like the 1964 Picturephone, Apple's FaceTime makes it possible to see in real time who we are speaking to. But unlike the Picturephone, it can be accessed from a digital device, either a cell phone or laptop computer, both of which can be transported and connected almost anywhere in the world. These same digital devices also provide us with the ability to work anywhere, research almost any topic, obtain answers to most any question, store the phone numbers and addresses of anyone we want to contact, guide us to our destinations, and take and store our photographs and videos. It is as though almost everything we need to function in this world can be done with, or found in our digital devices.

However, what these devices often fail to provide to us, what they can hinder us from attaining, and what they can sometimes actually contribute to us losing, is our real heartfelt connections to each other. It can often become too comfortable for people to post things on social media that they would not dare to say in person, to lose sight of the fact that these are real, live human beings on the receiving end of the posts. It can also become easier and more convenient to communicate via typewritten text or email rather than a voice-to-voice phone call, or even better, a face-to-face, heart-to-heart visit.

Indeed, the world has changed a great deal over the past half century, and technological advances are perhaps the most profound examples of these changes. These advances have brought many improvements to our lives and enabled us to communicate and connect in ways that are faster and broader than my eight-year-old mind could have ever imagined. But I believe it is of the utmost importance that while we utilize these innovative methods of interacting with each other, we remain mindful of their limitations. We must not allow these machines and man-made devices to alter our humanness. We cannot allow them to take the place of in-person conversations and contact. We must remember the vital roles that actual heartfelt communications with others, real-life dialogue, and interactions play in nourishing our souls and helping us to become more compassionate, loving, and empathetic beings. These human connections are what center us and ultimately help to define our humanity.

Coming Home

In October 2013, I made plans to visit friends who the previous year had moved from South Florida to North Carolina. I had decided to drive as this was a route I was very familiar with, and it suited my preference for traveling by car rather than plane. While I had made this road trip numerous times during the past several decades, this would be the first time that I was making it alone. It would be the first time since I was in my early twenties that I would be driving alone anywhere outside of the South Florida area.

Initially, I was hesitant about whether or not I should pursue this adventure. During my college years and the few years following college graduation, I made many long drives on my own. I thought nothing of driving alone from Miami to Gainesville, and even from Miami to Atlanta, Georgia, and Memphis, Tennessee. But that was three decades before, when I was much younger and quite a bit more daring. I was now middle-aged, and over time, had certainly lost a lot of my adventurous, risk-taking bravado.

As I debated over what to do, I sought the advice of my husband, Kevin, and my daughter, Jennifer. I was somewhat surprised that without any hesitation, they both encouraged me to make the trip. Kevin had known me since my late teens, so he was familiar with those earlier solitary ventures of my youth. Jennifer, who at the time was a few months shy of her twenty-seventh birthday, had grown up in a family where road trips, especially from South Florida to North Carolina, were commonplace. She also had become a young woman who was quite comfortable making her own solo drives. With their full support and confidence, I decided to hit the road. And I am so happy I did.

That trip to North Carolina took me out of my comfort zone and proved to be a wonderful experience. It opened my heart and profoundly stirred my creativity. And on my return, I felt a certain sense of calm and began a period of intense spiritual growth. My experience there sparked something deep inside me; it ignited a flame that burned within. I believe the fact that I allowed myself to make that solo road trip, something that I had not attempted to do for over three decades, provided me with a fresh perspective on what I was still capable of achieving. It reminded me of the independence I so often exhibited in my younger years. It also provided me a wonderful opportunity to spend quality time with some very special friends with whom I always have a lot of fun and engage in deep and meaningful conversations. When together, the three of us are never at a loss for words.

It was during this trip that for the first time, I shared a few of my writings with these friends. They encouraged me to continue writing and to consider compiling some of my work into a book format that could be shared with many people. Their encouragement played a pivotal role in my decision to embark on this creative journey. It provided the spark I needed to continue to put pen to paper and create the work displayed on these pages.

For whatever reason, in many ways unexplainable really, I feel such a deep connection to the beauty of the Blue Ridge Mountains and to the friends I visited while there. During that trip, I felt so energized, at ease, and peaceful. It is as though I had come home, reunited with places and people I had known for quite some time.

I believe that making the eleven-hour journey each way alone afforded me the opportunity to recapture a sense of adventure and independence that I did not even realize had been missing in recent years. By stepping outside my comfort zone, I was able to experience an awakening of parts of myself that had been lying dormant, perhaps buried just beneath the surface. I was now able to recognize more clearly my affinity toward those mountains and those friends. I was reminded that sometimes we must venture out in order to delve deep within and ultimately find our way home. Such experiences and relationships help to remind me of and believe deeply in God's eternal grace.

The Lessons of Daisy Doolittle

Daisy is the name of my cat, a female orange tabby, who will be turning six this summer. I have had a particular affinity for orange tabbies since my teenage years, when my family took in an orange male tabby we named Teddy. My mom was a real animal lover, so growing up, we always had animals in our home. I cannot remember a time when we did not have a dog. But in addition to a dog or two, we usually had a guinea pig, hamster, bird, or a tank full of fish to tend to. We even had a chicken for a very short period. But a cat was not one of the usual pets found in our home. Teddy was a sweetheart, though. He was docile and affectionate, and he remained a part of our family for several years.

In June 1983, Kevin and I were renting a house in South Florida. We had returned to the South Florida area a few months earlier, after I completed law school and passed the bar exam. One morning we noticed this tiny orange ball-like figure on the water's edge in the canal behind the house. Kevin went over and discovered this tiny little kitten, struggling to keep from slipping into the canal. He was able to pick him up and bring him into the house. He was so young and small that we had to bottle-feed him for those first few weeks. We named him PJ (Precious June), and like Teddy, he was a very affectionate, sweet, and docile feline. He was a member of our family for the next sixteen-and-a-half years.

A few years after PJ died, we ended up taking in two more orange tabbies, whom we named PJ2 and Dodger, both male. And both continued the tradition of being sweethearts.

Then there is the story of Daisy. One late afternoon in August 2012, I was on the screened-in patio at my house, reading a book. I happened to glance up and noticed what looked like an orange cat scampering in the backyard bushes. At that time, we still had Dodger, so for a moment, I thought that perhaps I had seen him. But Dodger was an indoor cat who rarely went outside.

After confirming that Dodger was in fact in the house, I went outside to the area where I had spotted the cat, and I caught another glimpse of her. I noticed that she was small, a kitten, and as soon as she saw me coming toward her, she ran away. I went back into the house, put some of Dodger's cat food in a paper bowl, and brought it out to the spot where the kitten had been. She was gone, but I left the bowl with the food and went back to the patio. Several minutes later, she reappeared. I watched from afar as she ate the food. And when I tried to approach her, she again ran away.

The next day I went to the grocery store and bought kitten food. Every day I would put the food out, and she would eat it. I tried desperately to get closer to her. I wanted to pet her, pick her up, and take care of her. But each time I tried to approach her, she would hiss at me and run away. I had never had this problem before, not with an orange tabby. She was so cute, and I was scared for her, this young kitten vulnerable to the outdoor elements. Some nights I would leave the patio screened door open for her, offering her a haven from which to escape the torrential summer rains. Several of those nights I would peek out and see her sleeping peacefully on one of the cushioned patio chairs.

After about six weeks of our routine, I noticed her rubbing against the branches of one of our small bushes. Based on my previous experiences with cats, I knew this indicated that she was seeking some affection. While she still would not come to me, I bought a cat toy, a stick about two feet long with a feather on one end. She allowed me to pet her with it. After a few days of that contact, I thought she was ready to be held. But as soon as I picked her up, she hurled out of my arms, leaving me with several bloody scratches. For the next few weeks, we continued our routine of feeding and some playing/petting with the toy stick, but it was clear she did not want to come too close and certainly did not want to be held.

While I had resigned myself to the fact that this kitten would never be my indoor domestic pet, I knew I still needed to take her to the vet to be examined, and if it was determined that she was healthy, have the required shots administered and have her spayed. Kevin and I managed to lure her into the patio area, and with no way to escape, Kevin, after shielding himself from the sting of her nails with thick gardening gloves on his hands and a heavy jacket to cover his arms, was able to get her down from the screen panel that she had frantically climbed. We were then able to carefully place her into the pet carrier and transport her to the vet's office. When I returned to pick her up from the vet later that day, I was advised that she was healthy but was certainly feral. I was informed that she had climbed the walls as soon as the carrier door was opened, and they had to sedate her to conduct the examination. Another appointment was scheduled to bring her back a few weeks later, when she would be old enough to be spayed.

In the interim, this kitten and I maintained the same routine. I would feed her, and she would play a little with the stick toy, but she would still hiss if I came too close. It was still clear that she did not want to be picked up. On the date of that next appointment with the veterinarian, Kevin and I repeated the previous process and managed to successfully get her into the carrier. And then, the strangest thing occurred. When I went back the next day to pick up that feral kitten, who we by that time had named Daisy, the vet assistant told me that Daisy had been extremely tame during her pre-op and post-op procedures, a complete change from the untamed animal they had encountered during her previous visit.

I had been told before the spaying procedure that I would have to keep Daisy inside the house for a couple of weeks until she had healed. I wondered how I was going to be able to keep this wild kitten in the house. It turns out that I did not have to worry because the kitten I brought home from the vet that day was so temperamentally different from the unruly kitten we had put into the carrier the day before. This kitten, now spayed and given a clean bill of health, had somehow transformed into a calm, sweet animal that enjoyed being held, petted, and cuddled. Daisy showed no inclination of wanting to go back to her life outdoors. This little feline, who I like to affectionately refer to as Daisy Doolittle, had become like all four of my previous orange tabbies. It had taken more time and effort for us to get to that place of friendship and trust, but we had somehow gotten there. And for the past half-decade, little Daisy Doolittle has been a wonderful addition to our family.

That tiny kitten. That orange bundle of joy. That sweet and precious being that showed up in my life, I have come to believe brought with her many valuable lessons.

She has taught me that when we least expect it, when we stop trying to force things and allow life to unfold as it is destined to do, when we surrender to the natural flow of our existence, that which is meant to be—perhaps that which we have been searching for—suddenly appears and makes its presence known. Sometimes it catches us by surprise. Often, we are not even aware that it is what we have been seeking.

This little ball of striped fur, who even now as a fully grown adult tabby is demure and petite in physical size, has reinforced for me the truth behind the adage that "Patience is a virtue." She has shown me how, over time and through simple, consistent acts of kindness and compassion, an enduring relationship can develop as uncertainty, timidity, and fear transcend into vulnerability, trust, and love. She has provided an example of the importance of allowing our hearts to remain open, of surrendering to and not fighting against the currents of our life's tides.

Oh yes, I have come to regard this delicate feline, this gentle soul, as a profound presence who has acted as both teacher and friend. She has served as a conduit through which the spiritual teachings of love, presence, and patience can be better understood. To me, she represents the brilliance of, the perfection of the divinely constructed master plan.

Little Daisy Doolittle has helped to remind me of the importance of maintaining reverence for all life forms, the need to honor and respect all of God's creations, both great and small, and to remember that sometimes the greatest gifts really do come in the smallest of packages, and at the most unexpected of times. Healing of the heart, in its most profound sense, is always possible.

The Eyes

Eyes. Two small objects on the face, positioned above the nose, below the forehead, responsible for what many humans would describe as the most important of the five senses, the ability to see.

They appear in a few different colors and a variety of shades and shapes. They are the viewfinders that enable us to look out at the world in which we live, fine-tuned lenses through which we can appreciate the vibrancy and beauty of our natural surroundings as we navigate through the course of our ordinary days.

From the deep-blue-sea to the glistening snowcapped mountains to the bright red and yellow autumn leaves to the magnificent purple and orange sunset, no matter the season—winter, spring, summer, or fall—regardless of the time or type of day, whether morning or night, sunny or clear, our eyes provide us with the opportunity to enjoy this panoramic living-color showcase.

While revealing so much about the world to us via our sense of sight, the eyes also serve to reveal much about us to the outside world. Often referred to as the "windows to the soul," they can provide essential clues as to the essence of who we are. They are a prism through which much of what we think and feel is reflected, what makes us tick, what causes us pain, what brings us joy, what warrants our approval, our disapproval, or sheer dismay.

From tears flowing out of hurt or despair to those released during a touching or sentimental moment to the sparkle triggered by a sense of excitement or a twinkle that accompanies a playful mood, these tiny portholes provide clear nonverbal cues to a wide range of emotions. And as to our thoughts, how effective is a glare, glance, or stare in communicating what it is we think about a particular situation? No words are necessary to deliver a stern reprimand when the fact that we are not pleased with something someone—perhaps a loved one, maybe a stranger—has said or done. A simple glare will do the trick. Hence the popular expression, "If looks could kill."

By the same token, we do not have to say anything to express our appreciation for the kind action of another. A soft glance and a quick wink can speak a thousand words. And doesn't a simple stare serve as a telltale sign of our intrigue with, or contemplation about, someone or something? Indeed, so many messages are conveyed without the utterance of a single sound.

In addition to being a purveyor of sight and silent communicator of thoughts and feelings, the eyes also play a role as masterful storytellers, disclosing information about our lives thus far. The fine lines, crow's feet, and deeper set wrinkles and crinkles serve as barometers by which to measure the number of years spent in this earth school. Our eyes provide direct evidence of the effects of the natural aging process and signs that there have been trials and tribulations along the way. The spectacles often worn as we grow older offer further proof of the years that have come and gone, representative of the changes that our vision has incurred from that of our youth to that of the present moment, projecting a certain aura of wisdom and knowledge, a sampling of the benefits that do come with age.

And what about the eyes as useful tools in providing a glimpse into a person's character, a bird's-eye view into the core of who we are, truthful or deceptive, confident or insecure, superficial or sincere, engaged in the current encounter or distracted?

If we focus in, read between the lines, and pay attention to the signals, we can learn so much about who a person is by the eye contact that he or she does not make. And when we gaze into the eyes of a loved one, a spouse, a child, a parent, a friend, if we pause for a moment and look deep enough, do we not sense an inner knowing, an understanding, an awareness that we are seeing beyond the physical parameters of this human being? We are seeing down into the depths of their souls, the purest, deepest part of an individual.

Oh yes, the eyes, these highly personalized scopes unique to each of us. The reason two individuals can look at an identical scenario and see very different things. Underscoring the importance, when necessary, to sit back and attempt to see the situation from the other person's perspective, to see it through another's eyes, knowing that our paradigms, our realities, while perhaps similar, are not the same.

Indeed, these two objects appearing on the face, positioned between the nose and the forehead, are tiny in terms of standard units of measurement but supersized in terms of their significance in our daily lives. The profound impact that they have on our journeys here, the vital roles they play in shaping our interactions with and perception of the world, the people, places, and experiences within it, are immeasurable.

The Heart

The heart. That relatively small organ, a muscle about the size of a fist located to the left of the middle of the chest. It is responsible for receiving and pumping blood throughout our bodies, providing the body with the oxygen and nutrients it needs, while at the same time, carrying away unnecessary waste.

This tiny muscle is an essential force in our existence here in our three-dimensional world. Without our hearts beating, we humans fail to survive. When it stops, we, as physical, living, breathing beings, cease to function in this earth school.

In addition to its vital role in the physical aspects of our lives, the heart is also regarded as a key element in our emotional well-being. It is often said that our hearts are broken when someone or something we love leaves us or is taken from us. And it is our hearts that we are frequently told to pay attention to when we are seeking answers to life's most important questions and making decisions and choices in our daily endeavors.

In some spiritual ideologies, Eastern tradition labels the heart as the fourth chakra, referred to as the energy center of love, the source that connects us to the deepest, purest parts of ourselves and propels us to be more grateful, compassionate, and kind. The Bible, which serves as the foundation of Western religious traditions, mentions the word *heart* hundreds of times. And it has been said that the New Testament sees the heart figuratively as the center of the real person, the center of spiritual life.

Oh yes, sweetheart. While it may not be large in terms of tangible standards of measurement, it remains central to us on physical, emotional, spiritual, and symbolic levels. And as we continue moving forward on this journey, let us listen more intently to our hearts' calls. Let us pay closer attention to the wisdom and insight that this inner compass can provide. Let us strive to be heart-healthy in all aspects of our lives. The physical, by nourishing our bodies with good nutrition and exercise. The emotional, by surrounding ourselves with people we love and who love us, and by engaging in activities for which we have great passion. The spiritual, by being grateful for the many blessings in our lives and appreciating all the abundance bestowed upon us, continually seeking to find the sacred in the ordinary, and recognizing the presence of a divine power so much greater than ourselves.

If we do these things, our hearts can remain strong, and our souls can evolve more fully. Let us, through the wisdom of our hearts, remain an open vessel through which we can impart our unique gifts to this world. Let us allow our hearts to be the driving force guiding us further away from the darkness and steering us ever closer to the light.

Love

This strong bond. This deep connection. This inner knowing. This clarity. This ability to feel another's joy and pain. To really "get them" in the deepest, most profound ways.

An intensity that goes beyond our everyday perceptions of reality, of life in this earth school. It flows from our hearts and transcends time and space. It is that which we know to be true down to the innermost depths of one's core. Love is a form of grace best described as coming from a divine power far greater than oneself, reminding us that we are spiritual beings having a human experience.

Love brings out the best in us. It makes us want to give completely, to help, to share, to guide. It is often overwhelming, and its appearance in our lives so unexpected. But once there, once it makes its way into the fabric of our lives, love's presence and the profound impact it has on us cannot be denied. It adds sunshine to an otherwise cloudy day. It ignites a flame within us and makes us want to spread our wings and soar. It is the most powerful force in the universe. It is love—that which is so true and real and pure.

Parenting

Children learn more from what you are than from what you teach.

—W. E. B. DuBois

Parenting: I believe it is the role of a lifetime, the most profound role that any of us can play. It is presented to us without a script, playbook, or instruction manual to follow. There is no diploma or degree that we can obtain that certifies we are properly trained and ready to pursue this position. There is only on-the-job training. We must learn as we go.

As is true with all our life endeavors, we bring our unique skill sets, perspectives, and past experiences with us, and these will influence how we parent. No doubt we will make mistakes. We will look back and question whether we should have handled some situations differently. We must remember not to be too hard on ourselves. We need to realize that there is not only one correct way.

There is no perfect parent, and there is no perfect child. And if we have more than one child, we will learn quickly that no two children are the same. Although they may have been created from the same genetic pool and raised in the same household environment, they are separate and unique beings. Like us, they come into this world with certain attributes and inclinations. They have their talents as well as their deficits.

As parents, we are left with the never-ending questions, the continual seeking, and the perpetual pondering. What can we do to help our children develop the skills needed to function successfully in the world? What can we do to foster the desire in our children to be the best that they can be? How do we instill in them the motivation to want to use their God-given talents to make this world a better place? How much responsibility should we bear for their successes and their failures? Are we to blame for their shortcomings? Are we to be given credit for their accomplishments?

I believe that as parents, we must ultimately recognize that we can only help guide our children toward what we believe is the best directions for them. We can provide them with a strong moral compass and the necessary tools, but we must allow them to find their ways. They must chart their own courses. We must do our best to instill strong values within our children. We must strive to help them to become healthy, happy, generous, and empathetic human beings. We must stress to them the importance of speaking the truth and living all aspects of their lives with integrity. We must, of course, lead by example. We must walk the walk and not just talk the talk. We must show them that actions speak louder than words, and we must be impeccable with our words to teach them to be impeccable with theirs. But in the end, we must recognize that they are separate beings from us. We may have given birth to them and nurtured them throughout their growing years, but they are unique creatures who have their life lessons to learn and their footprints to impart on this earth.

Through it all, it is of the utmost importance that we provide stable physical and emotional environments for our children. They need to know that we are there for them always, forever, unconditionally, without question. They need to know that we are their soft places to land, their shelters from any of life's storms. We must make them feel that our hearts are joined with theirs, their sorrows are our pain, and their joys are our happiness. They must know that they are the most valuable treasures in our lives. We must give them roots and wings, a core foundation rooted in unconditional love and a strong value system, and the freedom to spread their wings and fly.

Soulful Connections

I define connection as the energy that exists between people when they feel
seen, heard, and valued; when they can give and receive without judgment;
and when they derive sustenance and strength from the relationship.

—Brené Brown

There are people with whom our paths cross that for some seemingly unexplainable reason touch our lives so deeply. There is a certain connection that we feel, a tugging at the heartstrings, that seems to transcend time and space. These relationships are perhaps best described as a spiritual, soulful connection, one that seems to take us beyond the parameters of our everyday world, pushing us into a higher realm.

So many encounters on our journey in this lifetime, yet so few touch us this deeply. It is an inner knowing, an overwhelming sense of connectedness to these people, a strong feeling that we have traveled together before and truly know each other's essence. There is a certain familiarity, a comfort level, a knowingness that defies explanation in the strictly physical world, in the narrow confines of this lifetime. The heart is opened; all flows so naturally and easily. We find ourselves willing to expose our vulnerabilities as the barriers that so often hold us back from fully expressing ourselves disappear, and thoughts, words, and feelings pour out from the depths of our souls.

These relationships, and the events that bring these special people into our lives, help us to continue to believe in a divine design so much greater than ourselves. They help us to truly feel and trust and know God's grace. We must pay attention and recognize when these soulful connections appear in the fabric of our ordinary lives and acknowledge how truly extraordinary they are.

SPIRITUALITY AND THE DIVINE

Throughout human history, since the earliest days of humankind's existence, the concept of spirituality—the divine—has been the subject of much discussion, debate, and far too often, violent disagreements. While all the established religious orders refer to some type of divine power, some force or being that is greater than our human selves, they often have very different ideas about what that power is and how we are supposed to connect with it. Many people today refer to themselves as spiritual but not religious, while many argue that true spirituality can only be attained through adherence to a specific formal religious doctrine.

I was brought up in the Jewish faith. My family belonged to a synagogue that identified as being part of the Conservative branch of Judaism. In the Jewish religion, there are three main branches or denominations: Reform, Conservative, and Orthodox. Each group has differences in its practices based on its interpretation of the Jewish laws. Reform is the least restrictive, emphasizing the Jewish ethical tradition over the strict obligations of Jewish law. Orthodox is the most restrictive, adhering to a strict understanding and observation of Jewish law. Conservative is regarded as a midpoint between the two.

As a Conservative Jew, I went with my family to synagogue on the High Holidays of Rosh Hashanah and Yom Kippur. On a few Friday nights or Saturday mornings during the rest of the year, we sometimes went to synagogue but primarily to attend the bar or bat mitzvah of a family member or friend. I attended Sunday school and Hebrew school for a few years and was confirmed when I was in the tenth grade. I grew up lighting the Hanukkah menorah during the eight days of Hanukkah, fasting on Yom Kippur, and gathering with grandparents, aunts, uncles, and cousins two nights every spring for Passover seder.

I have very fond memories of growing up in a household that observed the Jewish faith, but I have not continued to follow the religious practices of Judaism. Looking back, I realize that it is not the religious doctrine or formal schooling that I remember or cherish most. It is the joy and love that I felt being part of the traditional holidays and family gatherings. Most important, it is the values that my parents taught me, ones that they showed me by their example: honesty, love, kindness, acceptance, empathy, and compassion. My parents walked the walk. They did not simply talk the talk.

As I have continued my life's journey, I have found myself embracing and cultivating these values. I have come to realize how deeply ingrained they are within the core of my being, and I hope they can serve to define the very essence of who I am. These values emphasize the importance of treating each other as we would like to be treated, giving unto every other human being the respect, love, kindness, and compassion that we most desire for ourselves, and they are at the heart of established religious orders and spiritual practices. These shared values are evidence that, regardless of the labels we choose to attach to a specific practice, whether we call it religion, spirituality, or a reference to the divine, we are at our core more alike than we are different. As we seek answers to some of life's most profound questions, we recognize that we are all in this together and a part of something so much greater than ourselves.

Creative Expression

As I continue along this life journey, taking the time to explore my place within the world around me, I become more convinced that the landscapes of our lives are all parts of a predesigned program, one specifically mapped out for us in fine-tuned detail before our entrances into this earth school.

I believe that we each come into this world with unique talents and special gifts bestowed upon us by the almighty Creator. Among these are distinct creative abilities, parts of us that manifest outwardly in some form of artistic expression. Some people write, others sing, some dance, draw, paint, sculpt, act, and construct buildings. Whatever form a person's gift takes, each provides a conduit through which our inner voices can be expressed and shared, serving as reflections of the way we communicate with the world, how we speak to it, and how it resonates within us. There is an ethereal quality to it, a spiritual essence at its core, and a representation of the deepest, purest parts of ourselves, one that seems to permeate and transcend all aspects of our daily lives.

For me, writing has served as that creative outlet. I feel my writings provide a window to my soul. They are a lens through which others can see into my innermost depths. They are the conduit through which I can express and better understand the world and my place within it.

Just as is true within the confines of the natural world, one's creativity undergoes varying cyclical patterns, often shifting between ebbing and flowing. There are times when our creative juices are overflowing with new ideas, thoughts come flooding in, swirling rapidly in a seemingly unstoppable motion. Then there are periods when the creative spark recedes, drought sets in, and we feel motionless, finding ourselves void of any new material.

As in nature, there is a certain rhythm to it all, one that cannot be force-fed or dialed up on demand. We must accept and surrender to the shifts as they come and go. Just as the seasons change—the bareness of winter gives way to the fullness of spring, and the hot days of summer turn into the crisp, cool evenings of fall—so, too, do our creative energies wax and wane. We must be patient during the leaner, drier times, trusting that it is merely a temporary hiatus, a momentary retreat backward, knowing from experience that this too shall pass, that we will emerge from the current state of hibernation and will once again surge ahead in what may feel like a sudden feeding frenzy.

As we travel along our life paths, we will find certain people, places, and events that serve as inspirational fuel that spark a fire within us, igniting the creative flame simmering quietly beneath the surface. These muses often seem to appear when least expected. They catch us by surprise, touch our hearts deeply, and compel us to again put pen to paper—or in today's world, fingers to computer keyboard—paint to canvas, lyrics to music, body movement to dance. The dry spell is over. Our creative juices are flowing once more.

Faith

And whether or not it is clear to you, no doubt the universe is unfolding as it should. Therefore be at peace with God, whatever you conceive Him to be. And whatever your labors and aspirations, in the noisy confusion of life, keep peace in your soul. With all its sham, drudgery, and broken dreams, it is still a beautiful world. Be cheerful. Strive to be happy.

—Max Ehrmann

The above quotation is found in the poem "Desiderata," written in 1927 by the American writer, Max Ehrmann. I first read those words in 1974, when I, along with my classmates, was given a copy of "Desiderata" at our high school graduation. I have heard it referred to as, "a poem for a way of life," and I can certainly understand such a reference. The piece, in its entirety, provides what I believe to be a simple but extremely compelling recipe for living, a guide to help us navigate through the complexities of our everyday lives.

Over the past several decades, I have often turned to the message in that poem for inspiration and guidance. I have read the piece so many times that its words are etched in my memory. And it is the above-cited words from "Desiderata" that came to mind when, during some difficult life experiences (some of which will be discussed in more detail in later writings), I found myself seeking answers to the following questions: How on earth did we ever get involved in this situation? How did we allow this to happen?

I used to truly believe that if you do good, good things will happen in your life. If you live by the Golden Rule and do unto others the way you want others to do unto you, you will somehow be kept out of harm's way. A naive thought, I suppose.

Yet through it all, I still believe there is a reason for everything that happens in our lives. There are certain lessons we are destined to learn, and these sometimes-harsh life experiences are often the conduits through which we must learn these lessons. However, this does not mean that we must walk through life with blind faith and that we should not at times question why we must willingly accept these difficult circumstances. Sometimes we just get plain tired and begin to believe, for the moment, that good things do not always happen to good people, and perhaps the good guys don't always win in the end. Indeed, bad stuff does happen to good people. And yes, we do get tired and sometimes lose faith that there is something to be learned from everything life presents to us.

It is during such times that we need to step back, take a deep breath, and pause to seek out and understand the lessons being taught. In these quiet moments of reflection, we are reminded that what we are experiencing are merely temporary difficulties, minor inconveniences on our spiritual journeys. With this new insight, this renewed perspective, we can snap out of what we now recognize as a momentary funk. We are awakened once more to our hearts' calls. We hear that inner voice speaking to us from the deepest and purest depths of our souls, from the very core of our beings, reminding us that our faith must remain strong, and we must trust that in the end, good will ultimately prevail.

We must continue to do our parts, no matter how small or seemingly unimportant they appear to be. We must have faith that we are on the right course and that each hardship is a necessary obstacle that must be encountered along the path to our destinations.

The Flow

The flow. The natural rhythm of our lives. That peaceful feeling that runs through us. A sense of calm and inner harmony that overshadows the chaos and turmoil of our surroundings, creating a semblance of simplicity and balance. It transcends all the confusion and uncertainty of this often-complicated world.

By paying attention to our inner compass, by living in and appreciating the present moment, by allowing our instincts to guide us, and by listening to our hearts' calls, we can access that inner flow in our everyday endeavors. If we take the time to slow down, to be still, to quiet our minds, we place ourselves in a position of openness to and acceptance of the natural direction of our life journeys. We can glide gently down the stream, allowing the water's currents to carry us along. We are aware that our feet, while firmly planted on the ground, are at the same time moving steadily beneath us, continuing to proceed forward on the path that lies ahead.

As we become more in tune with the profound presence of this energy, as we learn to embrace it and recognize its significance in our lives, we become more deeply connected to our purest, deepest selves. As we heed this potent force, as we strive to remain within the ease of and surrender to this natural flow, we move further along on the evolutionary path of becoming more whole, divine, enlightened beings.

Grace

Grace. That inner knowing, that peaceful feeling. The true belief that all is right with the world. The knowledge that the universe is as it should be, just as it has always been and will continue to be. Grace is intangible and immeasurable. It cannot be manufactured or sold, but in many ways, it is so very real. When it comes within our reach, it must be appreciated and embraced.

Grace is what takes us from the physical to the spiritual. It transcends time and space. It defies all the chaos and confusion of this fast-paced, hectic world. It surrounds us with tranquility and harmony. It makes us believe that peace on earth is truly possible. It makes us want to spread our wings and soar.

I believe that grace should be defined as magic in its purest form. It is the soul made visible. It is what makes us feel that anything is possible. It is nothing short of miraculous. It is what brings us closest to experiencing heaven on earth.

In those moments when we are embraced by grace, we must offer a prayer to that which is so much more powerful than ourselves. We must give thanks for the opportunity to rejoice in the moment. We must realize that we are so very fortunate to have had the joyful experience of recognizing this potent force in our lives.

Here's to you, grace. I offer you my deepest gratitude and appreciation for your presence in my life. I shall never take you for granted. I will strive to maintain you as an integral force that guides me forward on this journey. For you, for these moments when you touch me so deeply, I am so very grateful.

God's Grace

The longer I live, the more I realize that everything in my life, all that I am, stems from God's grace.

As I take time to step away from the hustle-bustle of everyday routines, as I quiet my mind and sit back and observe the world around me, as I go on solitary runs and walks in the beautiful foothills of the Blue Ridge Mountains, I can see with great clarity that it is the grace of God guiding my every thought, my every mood.

It is here amid nature's finest—the tall trees, the wooded paths, the rustling leaves, the sprawling greens, and the vast variety of insects and animals wandering about—that I am truly able to connect with and appreciate the essence of nature's amazing force, which transcends every aspect of my being.

It is in the calm, peaceful solitude of these beautiful natural surroundings that I can hear the vibrant beating of my overflowing heart, one filled with a deep sense of gratitude for all the abundance that has been bestowed upon me, knowing that all of it is, and always has been, because of God's grace. Never earned, just freely and benevolently given.

I recognize that God is in every breath I take and have ever taken, every move I make and have ever made, from the simplest of pleasures and good fortune to the grandest of life events. Even the mishaps and periods of darkness encountered along the way have only been made possible because of this most precious gift from the Creator.

Grace. Finding us when we are lost. Affording us an opportunity to see when we have been blinded and restoring us to wholeness when we have felt most broken. God's grace. This amazing grace. How sweet it truly is.

Inner Knowing

How do we know that we know what we know?

Intuitive knowing, predetermined thoughts and feelings, an inner awareness, one that speaks to us from the very depths of our souls. A certain tugging, a gnawing at the heartstrings. A whisper.

Just as the tiny spider weaves its web, the caterpillar creates its cocoon, and the graceful bird flies back and forth slowly building its nest, so, too, do we humans respond intuitively to the call of activity in our daily lives. We find ourselves propelled by certain forces that seem in many respects beyond our conscious control or understanding.

We come into this world with certain talents and unique gifts that we somehow instinctively know we are meant to develop and share. While these attributes flow easily, we also encounter deficits that we must struggle through. It is difficult to explain the reasons for these contradictions in our physical beings, our strengths and weaknesses, and how they vary from person to person. But just as in nature, hidden beneath the surface is a sense that we somehow just know that we know, as though we are somehow being automatically piloted along. Like the insects and animals creating what they need to transform, protect, and survive; the sunrise and the sunset making their appearances every day; the seemingly effortless transition from day to night; the cyclical shifting patterns of the four seasons, wherein summer gives way to fall, fall to winter, winter to spring, so, too, do our lives move in what often appears to be a somewhat uncontrollable sequence of events—a continual cycle of highs and lows, ebbs and flows—allowing us to reap and sow along the way.

We must take the time to be still, to afford ourselves opportunities to quiet our minds, to pay attention to the wonder of our natural surroundings, and to appreciate the parallels between our lives and nature's bounty. As we rest in the stillness of Mother Nature and allow ourselves to soak in the wisdom and lessons that are so abundant throughout her magnificent landscape, we become aware of the deepest yearnings of our souls. Our creative juices are stirred, and we can tune in to, really listen, truly hear the inner voice crying from within, providing us the opportunity to grow into our best selves, to connect with the true essences of who we are and who we are destined to be. As we open our hearts to her, as we surrender to and stand in awe of the true wonder of her glory, we enter that sacred place within us where we feel the very profound presence of God.

May we recognize and appreciate that divine love has bestowed on us, and may we fully grasp with every ounce of our being, with all our hearts and souls, that we owe everything to God's grace. May we become a bit better able to understand and to get a glimpse of what it is that we know. This is my earnest prayer.

Guidance

These days, it is as though my soul has opened. I have awakened to the joy and beauty that surrounds me, and I feel deep gratitude for all the abundance within my life. I appreciate the quiet and the peace that solitude can bring. I am learning to listen more, to speak less, and to trust the inner voice that stirs within. I am moving forward with patience and thoughtfulness. I feel that I have indeed grown firmer, simpler, quieter, warmer.

Knowing that there is still so much left to learn. Accepting that there is still so much to be fearful of and to worry about in this often harsh and complicated world. Yet, throughout all the confusion and concern, I feel a certain serenity flowing through me these days.

In some ways, I often feel that I am a bystander, watching the world speeding by at a frenetic pace. It is as though I am somewhat detached from so much of the common chaos and hustle-bustle of daily life.

These past couple of years have been a time of deep reflection, a period consumed by much thought and prayer. It had suddenly become so crystal clear that certain things were no longer working in my life, and I knew I had to seize the opportunity to make necessary changes. There was an inner knowing that told me I had to shift my thinking and pushed me to focus on my real priorities.

Looking back, I want to describe the clarity, the shift, as a force that was so much greater than me. A part of me and yet at the same time a power so much larger than me, perhaps best described as very strong spiritual guidance. The guidance that led me to this path seems so natural, so right. The feeling that my life has changed direction. Grateful that it has shifted to follow this course. Knowing that there is still so much to learn, so many ways in which to grow, and so many hardships to endure.

Believing that there are no coincidences, that life is unfolding as it must, as it is predestined to do. Trusting that I will continue to move forward and be able to remain balanced amid the ebb and flow of everyday life. Understanding that love and truth must be my guide. For all of this, and for my life, I am so grateful.

Karma

Everything you done to me, already done to you.

—Celie, in *The Color Purple,* by Alice Walker

Karma. A word linked to the concept that for every action there is a reaction. Sir Isaac Newton codified the idea as it pertained to the physical world in his third law of motion: "For every action, there is an equal and opposite reaction." In the spiritual realm, this idea has come to be referred to as karma. It is the spiritual principle of cause and effect, where the intent and actions of an individual (cause) influence the future of that individual (effect). The belief that good intentions and good deeds contribute to good karma and future happiness, while bad intentions and bad deeds contribute to bad karma and future suffering.

I have given this concept of karma a great deal of thought over the past several decades. I have come to think of it as being closely linked to the Golden Rule of, "Do unto others as you would want others to do unto you," and the idea that "What goes around comes around."

I believe we too often lose sight of this important principle. In our quests for material wealth, our desires to control others, to prove that we are "better than," we cease treating each other with the respect, compassion, and humanity that we are all worthy of. Our egos become the driving force behind our daily actions and communications, and we find ourselves consumed by the trappings of external power. We resort to whatever means we feel are necessary to achieve our goals. We convince ourselves that the end justifies the means and dismiss thoughts questioning the moral barometer of those means.

We need to recognize that, while this disregard for how our actions affect others, this desire to get ahead, to achieve regardless of the cost, may provide us in the short term with satisfactory results, in the long run, we will find that we have paid a far too high price. While the immediate payout may seem worthwhile, able to sustain us while feeding our ego-driven selves, we will come to realize that in the process, we have starved our authentic selves. In the grand scheme, the big picture, there will be consequences for our actions, and we will be forced to pay back any overage we have received. As the character, Celie, in Alice Walker's Pulitzer-winning book, *The Color Purple,* so succinctly and dramatically states, "Everything you done to me, already done to you."

Such is this spiritual principle of karma. For every action there will be a consequential reaction. Our intentions and actions determine what those reactions will be, whether positive or negative. Our karmic balance is continually readjusting.

Meditation

Meditation, in all its forms and traditions, is an invitation to listen, to open,
to quietly enlist the courage to be touched and formed by life.

—Mark Nepo

Meditation. A time of reflection, of quiet, of peace. A time to be still, to listen, to travel deep within. It is an opportunity to silence the chatter that constantly runs through our minds and to break free from the many distractions that consume so much of our everyday thought processes. It allows us to connect with the deepest, purest parts of ourselves, to reunite with our true essence, and to remind us of the wonderful spiritual beings that we are.

Incorporating meditation into our everyday routines, making the commitment to have it become a necessary part of our daily rounds, enables us to focus more intently on the beauty that surrounds us. It allows us to see with greater clarity the world that we are in but not of. It helps us to think less and feel more, to tune in to intuition, that inner knowing, that sense that all is as it should be, as it always has been, and will continue to be. It reminds us to remain open, to stay calm, and to allow our hearts to be the vessels that carry us forward on this journey.

Meditation serves as a means through which we can learn to live in the flow of life, to pay attention, and to heed the natural rhythm of our lives. Living in this flow helps us to become more joyful, compassionate, peaceful, and loving beings. It creates within us a sense of ease and wonder that can then be projected to the outside world as a joyful presence, a lightness of spirit, an aura of tranquility and calm.

Meditation provides a pathway to continue moving toward the light and distancing ourselves from the darkness. What we focus on expands, and as we quiet our bodies and our minds, as we become still and concentrate on the inhalation and exhalation of our breath, we are reminded of the true essence of who we are and the absolute magnificence of all that we are designed to be.

Mindfulness

To live a mindful life. To think before we speak or act. To understand the intentions behind all that we say and do.

To pay attention to our surroundings. To be attentive to the people we encounter.

To really be there, present in every moment, no matter how inconsequential that moment may seem.

To live a mindful life is to be a part of all that is going on around us.

To truly see the beauty of nature's bounty. To listen intently to the conversations in which we are engaged.

To allow ourselves to be present in the here and now. To remain openhearted and receptive to the many messages that come our way.

To look people in the eye, attempting to really see and understand what is behind their words and actions, and at the same time, to remain mindful of the motives behind ours.

Music

Music provides food for the soul, nourishment for the heart,

A melody or a lyric that resonates deeply within us right from the start.

It has the unique ability to perk us up when we are feeling down,

To create a smile from what had been a frown.

It conjures up memories of days gone by

As it reminds us of times when we would laugh or cry.

Whether it be classical, jazz, pop, country, rock, or Broadway,

It has a way of bringing sunshine to an otherwise cloudy day.

No matter the genre or the language in which it is sung,

It offers an opportunity to connect each of us to every other one.

Some music is composed of words that tell stories; some have no words at all.

But whether lyrics or melody only, it manages to tune us into our heart's call.

Music can break down our human barriers and play a vital role

In bringing us together, soul to soul.

My Prayer

Use me, God. I want to serve. I want to help. Please guide me in my search to discover and share my unique gifts in my everyday endeavors and encounters. Help me to remain humble, openhearted, open-minded, compassionate, and kind. Allow me to radiate light and love into this universe of which I am a part. Remain alongside me on this journey as I strive to be the change I want to see in the world. Provide me with the inner wisdom and peace to stay hopeful and faithful.

Continue to grace me with your divine presence so that I may truly feel your love, your light in every facet of my life, knowing that you are offering me your comfort and protection even during times of apparent darkness and despair. Help me to continue to seek, find, and truly appreciate the sacred in the ordinary. Show me the way that I can best be of service to you and to my fellow man.

Lead me along the path of carrying out my purpose for being in this life, at this time. And please know, dear God, I give you my word that where you lead, I will follow.

Spirituality

I have never considered myself to be a religious person. In fact, I seem to feel no real affinity toward any organized religious faith or institution. And yet, I am aware of a strong spiritual connection that transcends every aspect of my daily life.

As I have taken the time to slow my speed of life, speaking less and listening more, doing less and being more, I have come to realize just how powerful this force is in my life. It is not tied to any formal religious training. It goes far beyond any formal doctrines that I have been taught. It is an innate part of my existence. It flows so fluidly throughout my being. It somehow guides my every act and thought.

For me, spirituality is a certain knowingness within my soul. It provides me with a strong value system and a firm belief in what is right and what is wrong. It helps me find my way when the path becomes confusing. It offers comfort when sadness fills my heart. It speaks to me in screams and whispers when I'm not paying attention and whispers little pearls of wisdom when I am ready to listen. Spirit, you are my guide, my love, and my rock.

Spiritual Fuel

Some people, some places, and some experiences invigorate us, inspire us, and feed our spirits. Some deplete us, drain us, and zap our energetic flows. Some merely numb us, neutralize us, and leave us feeling nothing at all.

The mixture of emotions that pass through us varies from one person to the next. Often, we cannot explain our reactions to the circumstances confronting us. We are not sure of the reasons behind these shifts; why some individuals, environments, or events lift us higher, fill us up, and draw us out. Others drag us down, empty our tanks, cause us to withdraw back into and perhaps never leave our protective shells.

There do not appear to be simple answers to these most basic questions. These emotions, or lack thereof, remain a mystery. Another of life's perplexing puzzles that we find ourselves pondering over, wondering about. Perhaps one that we will never be able to solve in this lifetime, in this earth school.

Maybe we must forgo our attempts to understand why some pieces fit so easily, lining up almost perfectly with one another, while others just don't quite match, the edges continually out of alignment. Should we not learn to accept the uncertainty of it all, realizing that the fragments are falling into the order that is best for our journeys in this place at this time?

Trusting that all is part of the divine grand scheme, the master plan that has been designed specifically for us, our unique jigsaw puzzles—misfits, broken pieces, and all. Surrendering to the ebb and flow of our heart's calls. Having faith that with God's grace, we are provided with just the right amount of spiritual fuel needed to reach our desired destinations.

Spiritual Peace

Spiritual peace. A form of grace. An inner knowing that all is well, that the universe is as it is designed to be, and our lives within it are unfolding as they are destined to do. It is a contented stillness of the soul that manifests outwardly as a calm, peaceful, and joyful presence, a state of ease that permeates one's entire being, a feeling of deep connection to and a rhythmic flow with the world of which we are a part. It is a powerful sense that we are one with all life forms, no greater than or less than any of God's magnificent creations with which or whom we share this planet.

It stirs within us a desire to approach our daily endeavors with a certain mindfulness, to pay attention to our every thought and action, to slow down, to observe, to listen, to attempt to see and feel the essence of all that we say and do. It compels us to remain conscious, to stay awake, and to appreciate the gifts offered in the present moment, providing the opportunity to simply be tuned into the pulse, the energy that exists in all that surrounds us.

Spiritual peace is the place where unconditional love is birthed. It is the truth of the soul, a perception of the world fueled by a natural clarity, an innate awareness, an effortless unfolding of all that is and of all that we are meant to be. It is a state of being wherein we speak and act with compassion, humility, and kindness, all flowing from a place of love rather than fear. The Bible refers to it as the peace that passes all understanding. Spiritual peace, perhaps the closest we can come to experiencing heaven on earth.

Trusting as We Seek

Getting found almost always means being lost for a while.

—Anne Lamott

I am experiencing a certain longing, an aching, a sadness, a pull. A melancholy feeling of sorts. A bit lost these days as waves of confusion gnaw at my soul. Perhaps best described as a period of seeking, of longing to find and understand the purpose of it all. Of realizing that there is so much to learn, so many ways in which to grow, and wanting to break free of all the madness and uncertainty. My heart's desire is to not feel so unsettled and confused.

Recognizing that just as the seasons come and go, so do our lives ebb and flow. The dark cold of winter gives way to the bright warmth of spring. The vibrant greens of summer turn into the golden leaves of fall.

I am yearning to maintain a sense of peace throughout the changes as they occur. Wanting to truly grasp the essence of it all. Understanding that life is not static and that there will inevitably be highs and lows along the way. Trusting that all is as it is designed to be. That a power far greater than ourselves, perhaps one that we can never truly comprehend in this lifetime, is working in us, through us. This power is guiding our every move, leading us forward, and carrying us along on our journeys.

Surrendering to this force. Giving ourselves freely, completely, to this indescribable presence. One that transcends time and space. One that defies rational thought and logic. One that reaches down and takes hold of the deepest parts of us, that latches on to and touches the very core of who we are, and that awakens our spirits and moves us to the most profound depths of our beings. That which tugs at our hearts and souls continually seeking to bring us ever closer to the light. Trusting in the magnificent Source of all love as we continue seeking on our journeys.

Unknowing

In the beginner's mind there are many possibilities, but in the expert's there are few.

—Shunryu Suzuki

There are some things that we just cannot explain.

Feelings that we have, connections that we make, thoughts that permeate our minds. Why do some people, places, or experiences touch us so deeply?

What is it about a relationship that makes it so special? What is the significance of that person's presence in one's life? What is the meaning of a specific experience we are having, and why has this situation presented itself now? What is the reason behind this chapter? What role will this play in the larger scheme of life? What lessons are being taught? What picture is being painted? What story is being written? What song is being composed?

The unknowingness of it all. The uncertainties presented. Yet through it all, trusting that regardless of the outcome, it is a project we must pursue as the force of the pull is far too powerful to ignore. It tugs so heavily at our heartstrings. It touches us down to the innermost core of our beings. It seems to come from a source so much greater than oneself. It transcends time and space as we know it in this three-dimensional world of which we are a part.

We must step back and detach ourselves from it, while at the same time, opening ourselves completely to it. Allowing it to flow through us, to run its course, to carry us forward on this journey. We must surrender to the unknowingness, trusting that it is a necessary part of the master plan, knowing deep inside us that all is as it is meant to be.

VIRTUES

VIRTUES

The concept of virtue has been widely referenced from the earliest of biblical times through today, both in secular and nonsecular domains. The word itself is generally defined as behavior exemplifying high moral standards; a trait or quality that is deemed to be morally good. While there is no singular definitive list of virtues, there is consensus that certain characteristics and actions clearly fit in this category and are deemed worthy of being included in any such list. Patience, humility, compassion, empathy, kindness, honesty, forgiveness, and gratitude are a few examples.

As I have continued on my life's path, seeking to understand more about myself and the world around me, I have come to realize the vital role these recognized virtues have played, and continue to play, in my growth process. I have learned to value how applying these virtues in my life expression has helped me to become my best self, my truest self, my most authentic self.

I believe that if we humans, as a collective whole, incorporate more of these simple virtues into our everyday lives, if we take the time to pause and with patience really listen, truly attempt to understand and allow ourselves to feel real empathy for another's pain, learn to forgive the indiscretions of those who have hurt us, and treat each other with kindness and compassion, then perhaps we will be worthy of the wise words of Mahatma Gandhi: "Be the change that you wish to see in the world."

Gratitude

Gratitude is not only the greatest of virtues, but the parent of all others.

—Marcus Tullius Cicero

If the only prayer you ever say in your entire life is—Thank You—it will be enough.

—Meister Eckhart

Throughout my journey, I have come to regard gratitude as perhaps the most transformational force in my life. It is the foundation from which all the other positive principles seem to flow. When we are grateful for the simple blessings in life, when we view our lives as abundant rather than lacking, we naturally become more patient, empathetic, compassionate, and kind.

My first recollection of becoming acutely aware of the power of gratitude was in 1996, when I read Sarah Ban Breathnach's book *Simple Abundance: A Daybook of Comfort and Joy.* I had recently celebrated my fortieth birthday and was working full time as an attorney while raising my three children, who were then ages ten, six, and four. Needless to say, between carpools, children's school and social functions, all other everyday motherhood and household responsibilities, and running a law firm, I was extremely busy and often felt as though I could hardly catch my breath. Multitasking was a way of life, and downtime was not a phrase that had a place in my vocabulary. It was during that time I saw an article in the local paper that talked about Oprah Winfrey and her recommendation of Sarah Ban Breathnach's book. I was, and still am, a big fan of Oprah, and although during those busy days I had not been taking much time to do pleasure reading, there was something in that article, something about Oprah's description of why she felt it so important a book to read, that stirred my curiosity enough that I made a trip to the nearest bookstore and bought my copy.

The book consists of short essays, one for each day of the year, that remind us of the importance of pausing amid our hectic, chaotic daily lives to soak in and appreciate the beauty that is all around us, to find joy in the simple pleasures, to seek the sacred in the ordinary, and to focus on the abundance rather than the lack in our lives. And, at the core of these reminders was the importance of being grateful.

The book hit home for me. It was music to my ears, nourishment for my soul. It awakened something in me. It seemed to be just what the doctor ordered, a prescription offered as a cure for an illness I did not even realize I had. And I found her emphasis on gratitude particularly powerful. Ban Breathnach suggested that we write down five things each day that we are grateful for and published *The Simple Abundance Journal of Gratitude* to help facilitate this process. I purchased the journal and began the routine of logging in five per day. I found this simple process transformational. I discovered that on most days, finding five was easy. And I found myself expressing gratitude for the simplest of blessings.

It became clear to me that there are so many things to be grateful for every day, and the simple things matter most. The special people within our lives. Those with whom we can connect and confide. Our five senses—to be able to see, hear, touch, taste, and smell. I found myself having a particularly renewed appreciation for the way our senses enable us to experience all that surrounds us, recognizing that without any one of them, the richness of life is severely altered. I became more acutely aware of how fortunate we are to be able to gaze in awe at the sight of a beautiful sunset, to be enamored by the sweet melodic sound of a bird's song, to be invigorated by the scent of the gardenias blooming in the garden, to feel the needles of the pine tree softly tickling our palm, to be awakened and nourished by the flavor of the ocean's salty waters. These precious gifts offered to us by our senses are simple treasures to behold and should never be taken for granted. Rather, they should be appreciated with reverence and grace.

I also found myself expressing gratitude for such simplicities as a fresh cup of morning coffee, a hot shower, an enjoyable meal, a good conversation with a family member or friend, having enough money to be able to pay monthly bills, feeling pain-free on a run, sunshine, crisp mountain air. The list goes on and on. It is remarkable how much there is to be thankful for in what is so often regarded as the seemingly mundane aspects of our daily lives.

Over two decades later, I still purchase a new journal each year, and on most days, I make my five entries. More important, even if I do not log them in the journal, I seem to make a mental note of them every day. I have found that gratitude remains at the front and center of my daily life, and even during difficult days, trying and painful times, I do my best to look up and search for the sunshine sometimes obscured behind the dark clouds.

When we adopt an attitude of gratitude in our daily lives, we find ourselves seeking out and recognizing the extraordinary in the ordinary. We find that even when adversity and turbulence surround us, and on the surface life appears uncertain and unkind, the attitude of thankfulness that has become such an integral part of our being helps to sustain us. It provides us with an inner knowledge that this too shall pass. It reminds us that although the waters on the surface of our lives are rough and rocky, below the surface, the waters remain calm, and tranquility abounds.

As we travel through life on this journey, we must allow gratefulness and gratitude to be our guide. Gratitude stabilizes our inner compasses. It brings humility and balance to our lives. We must awaken each day and give thanks for another day of living. We must lie down to sleep each night and give thanks for all that was bestowed upon us this day.

Acceptance

I may never be healthy on paper but I am well.

—Kris Carr

I t was in the fall of 2013 that I first heard the above statement by Kris Carr during an episode of Oprah's *Super Soul Sunday*. Carr was Oprah's guest that day, and she was speaking about her life since being diagnosed with a rare stage IV cancer ten years prior. With the diagnosis came the prognosis that the cancer was incurable and untreatable and that it carried a life expectancy that would not exceed ten years. Carr explained how for the first few years following her diagnosis, she would go to her follow-up scans and doctor appointments with the mindset that she was broken unless and until the medical professionals could tell her she was perfectly healthy. She went on to say that she soon realized that if she did not change her thinking, she would be chasing this dragon for the remainder of her life. It was then that she made the conscious decision that regardless of what the medical tests and professionals revealed, she would be okay. She would not regard herself as broken because she would be living life well. Her newly adopted attitude became as the eleven-word epigram expresses, "I may never be healthy on paper but I am well."

The Carr interview, especially those simple eleven words, really resonated with me. In January 2011, I was diagnosed with scleroderma, an autoimmune disease that, like Carr's cancer, is rare and incurable. There are a few forms of the disease, and mine, known as diffuse systemic sclerosis, is generally considered the most severe. The condition is characterized by the buildup of scar tissue (fibrosis) in the skin and other organs. In my case, the disease was progressing rapidly, and there was a significant risk of damage to internal organs.

By the time of Carr's appearance on *Super Soul Sunday*, I had been battling the disease for nearly three years. I was being treated with heavy doses of prescription medications and seemed to have the disease under control. As I listened to Carr speak about her ten-year journey living with her diagnosis, I recognized many similarities between her experience and my own.

Like Carr, before my diagnosis, I had never heard of my disease. When I was first diagnosed and began to do some online research, I learned this was a death sentence, probably within five years. Until then, I would likely experience debilitating physical impairment.

As I informed friends and family about my diagnosis, they were, of course, deeply concerned and saddened. But the most common response was something along the lines of, "How could this happen to you? You are the healthiest person that I know."

I was not completely surprised by this response because, since my early twenties, I had lived a healthy lifestyle. I ran six to seven days a week and maintained a healthy diet. So while I understood their reactions, I never thought that way. I would respond by saying something like, "This can happen to anyone. Adopting a healthier lifestyle does not guarantee that a person will not become ill. It is just a matter of doing what you can to hopefully feel better each day that you are alive and perhaps ward off some diseases in the process."

What I did not say, but what was a key thought I had from the first day of my diagnosis through today, is something I read several years before being diagnosed with scleroderma: When we experience hardship, the question should not be, "Why me?" but rather, "Why not me?" To me, the rationale behind this statement—that despite our best intentions and actions, none of us should expect to be exempted from life's inevitable difficulties—is one that clearly impacted the lens through which I viewed my life-threatening diagnosis. This perspective enabled me to accept the curveball thrown at me, refrain from pity-me parties, recognize that some things were clearly beyond my control, and move forward determined to fight this opponent head-on. And fight I did.

From the initial diagnosis in January until October of that same year, I went to several doctors, talked to a few people who were battling the same disease, and did a lot of research. My inclination toward a healthier, more natural lifestyle made me leery of prescription drugs. I truly believed at first that the body was capable of healing through natural remedies and that this was the path to wellness I needed to pursue. During those initial ten months, I sought alternative approaches, which included herbs provided by a Chinese medicine practitioner, vitamins, minerals, and supplements recommended by an integrative medical doctor, adherence to a strict vegan diet, and juicing every day. By October, it was obvious that none of my natural remedies were sufficient. The disease was progressing rapidly, as evidenced by the fibrosis that now extended from my face to my feet.

I concluded that it was time to seek a more traditional approach. I made an appointment with a doctor at the University of Pittsburgh Medical Center (UPMC), who was one of the leading specialists in the treatment of this disease. I was placed on two drugs, both quite potent. And as with all medications, both came with a lengthy list of potential side effects. The medications did seem to help, and within a few months, the fibrosis started to subside; the disease appeared to cease progressing.

For the past six and a half years, I have continued to take my daily meds, the dosages of which have been slowly reduced. Twice a year I venture back to Pittsburgh for follow-up visits with the specialists at UPMC. Between visits, I have appointments with other specialists closer to my home in South Florida to make sure that internal organs such, as the heart, lungs, and kidneys, are functioning properly. Lab work is done every three months to check that my body is still tolerating the drugs. I am grateful that thus far, the lab reports have not shown any signs of rejection of the medications. And other than some esophageal issues and contractures of the joints in my hands, there is no evidence of impairment to other organs.

I feel gratitude each day for the quality of life I am able to experience. While I continue to do my part in maintaining a healthy lifestyle of good nutrition and daily exercise, I recognize this is an incurable disease whose course could be altered at any time in a direction and in ways beyond my control. I have accepted that living with this medical condition is my new normal. And like Kris Carr, while I may never be healthy on paper, I am well.

Looking back, I have come to realize the vital role that acceptance has played in the vantage point from which I have approached my life-threatening and life-altering diagnosis. My decision from the beginning, whether conscious or not, to battle this illness from the broader life perspective of accepting what is, rather than focusing on what I want it to be, enabled me to absorb some important life lessons. The health obstacle that had suddenly been placed in my path taught me to recognize the necessity of moving forward, not looking back, and perhaps most important, not to dwell on, "Why me?" It is what allowed me to grasp so deeply the positive message behind Kris Carr's words long before I ever heard her say them. And it is why that simple phrase, "I am well," resonated so profoundly with me once I did. Acceptance: What a powerful and transformational gateway to personal healing.

Ego vs. Humility

have believed for quite some time that ego is the driving force behind most of the world's problems. It is the ego that causes human beings to want to win at all costs, to be the best, to have the most, and to control completely.

Egotistical people too often forget the Golden Rule. They lose sight of the effects their actions have on those around them. The art of winning, the strategy of the game, becomes all-consuming. They do not pause to examine the motives behind their actions. They are convinced that the ends justify the means, and too often, they do not even question the means.

I believe it is the ego-driven part of human personality that leads to violence, war, intolerance, and the placement of too great an emphasis on materialistic aspirations and achievements. It fuels an environment where people pass judgment on each other, where labels of "us" and "them" become all too common, and where an individual's worth is often measured by the material wealth he or she possesses.

If only ego would take a back seat for a while and allow its alter ego, humility, to take the wheel. Perhaps then we would no longer be driven by the desire to be the best, to have the most. Perhaps then we would realize that in the grand scheme, material wealth and the trappings of external power derived from our ego-driven actions have no intrinsic value. Having the most possessions, the grandest title, and the most control does not make one the worthiest. True worth, real value, and authentic power cannot be measured by such superficial means.

If we were to approach our daily endeavors with a sense of modesty and humbleness, if we were to strive to be the best that we can be but not at the expense of others, if we were to do good deeds without expecting a pat on the back or some glorified recognition, if we really set aside our ego-driven tendencies, I believe we could transform the world. I believe that the natural consequence of actions based on less ego and more humility is a society fueled by and overflowing with mutual respect, compassion, kindness, empathy, and love. Ego vs. humility? As always, the choice is ours.

Integrity

ntegrity: being whole; unbroken; an absence of fighting within one's self; a lack of controversy between the two halves of a person's soul. These are some of the definitions used to define the word *integrity*.

As I have grown older and perhaps more introspective, I have found myself giving quite a bit of thought to this word and what it means within my life and the lives of others. I have come to believe that integrity lies at the very core of the quest for personal peace and harmony. It flows from within and extends outward to the external environment. It is an inner knowing; a sense of karmic balance; a warm, steadfast current that flows peacefully through us. It speaks to us firmly. It guides us in setting the parameters of what is right and what is wrong. It brings us together with our authentic selves. It is when the personality is in alignment with the soul.

I am convinced that when we live outside our integrity, we violate our internal compasses, and we disrupt all that is right within ourselves. I believe it is this disruption that leads to wars, hate, violence, and intolerance. It is a diversion from one's center. It is driven by ego, and it causes a division in our souls.

The life of someone of integrity may not be easy, but it is simple. A person of integrity knows which course he or she must follow. When a fork in the road is encountered, a person of integrity knows which path to take. That inner voice speaks in decibels above all other distractions. Although temptations may be present, to the person of integrity, they are but fleeting thoughts. They are never truly tempting. They are never really considered viable alternatives. A person of integrity is guided by that inner knowing, a firm, unyielding foundation upon which his or her karmic balance is grounded.

I believe that it can truly be so very simple. Not always easy, but simple. And so I shall this day make a vow to strive to stay within the bounds of my integrity. To listen to that inner voice. To remain unbroken in all aspects of my life: physical, emotional, and spiritual. I shall treat my body as a temple. I shall nourish it with good nutrition and exercise. I shall seek to listen to my heart's call, to allow my love and inner knowing to be my guide. I shall give thanks for all the wonderful people in my life. I shall express gratitude for the ability to hear, see, touch, taste, and smell all that surrounds me. I shall continue to strive to be the best that I can be and to remain true to my integral core. It may not be easy, but it truly is so very simple.

Kindness

In a world where you can choose to be anything, choose to be kind.

—Jennifer Dukes Lee

first saw the above statement imprinted on a shirt in the gift shop of a local church. I was intrigued by this fourteen-word phrase, and I just had to buy the shirt. Such simple words, but what a profound message. I have worn that shirt often in the months since my purchase and have now sought other products containing this same phrase.

Long before I purchased the shirt, I had given quite a bit of thought to the concept of kindness. For many years, I have kept a copy of the book *Random Acts of Kindness* (by the Editors of Conari Press) on display in the small office space in my home. I have come to regard kindness as one of the most important virtues. I have seen the powerful impact of a kind word or deed. Kindness can open hearts and change minds. It brings out feelings of, or perhaps is born out of, compassion, empathy, and love. I believe that in our modern-day society, in the politically charged and divisive environment we are currently experiencing, we need it more than ever. Kindness—along with compassion, empathy, and love—is essential to retaining our humanity.

The following is a short poem that I wrote over a decade ago. It is quite basic, but like the phrase on that shirt, in a world where we can choose to be anything, how wonderful would it be to start with the simple act of choosing to be kind?

Kindness

Small acts of kindness each and every day,

Adding a little smile in a very simple way.

What a different world this place might really be,

If each one of us looked beyond the me, me, me.

Think about the way our lives could shine with quite a bit more light,

If only we would use our gifts and simply do things right.

If only we could take away the meanness and the hate

And replace them with love and kindness,

Now would that not be just great?

Perhaps I am a dreamer.

Some would say I ask too much.

Others would say to expect these things is completely out of touch.

Yet deep down inside me, I feel so very sure

That this is what we must really seek

To be simple, kind, and pure.

And so, I will attempt to contribute in my own special way

By doing something nice for another every single day.

A little act of kindness—

A word, a look, a call.

Such a tiny effort really,

But what great things can grow from seeds so very small?

Patience

Patience. Something I have learned quite a bit about these days. A very important virtue, it is vital in achieving a more spiritual life. It means taking things slowly, one step at a time, and understanding that we must walk before we run. We must listen carefully before we speak. We must think seriously before we act. We must allow time to be our friend and haste to become our foe.

It is with patience that we are best able to accept the challenges that life inevitably brings our way, seek the meaning behind the adversity, and evolve more fully from the lessons being taught.

Ah yes, patience, a very important ally these days. A gift time allows us. A treasure to be embraced with grace and gratitude. A very important virtue indeed. Be patient, stay focused, be grateful, and good things will come.

Priorities

How did the world's priorities get so messed up? Where did we go so very wrong? How did we get to this place?

I do not know the answers.

There is so very much I do not profess to know these days.

But of one thing I am quite certain:

To survive this mayhem, we absolutely must change our ways.

I truly believe this from the innermost depths of my soul,

That the world is meant to be a peaceful place.

And to that end, man can play a key role.

I pray that we can get through this, and that awaiting us shall be a better life,

A place of love and harmony,

An environment of no war and strife.

I think we are at a crossroads.

We must decide which path we want to take.

We must reevaluate all our priorities,

Decide what is real and what is fake.

The material possessions that have sustained us,

The technology that has grown and grown,

Throughout all this supposed progress,

The seeds of hate and mass destruction have been sewn.

We must strive to go back to basics,

To make the world a better place.

A world where children can grow and prosper

With smiles and laughter encompassing their face.

Oh, please let us not waste this opportunity.

We must see to it that all this evil does fail.

Man must realize that it is through love, compassion, and kindness, that good can once and for all prevail.

Simplicity

For quite some time now, I have said the world is way too complicated for me. I do not know when I first began to feel this way. I am not sure why I found myself using that expression. I do know that I have never been more certain of its truth.

I have spent these past months attempting to simplify my life and regain some semblance of control over my everyday world. I have shifted my focus from racing through life to slowing down several notches. I have been focusing more on hearth and home. I have been listening more intently to my inner voice. I have been doing more of what I want to do rather than merely what is expected of me. I have been stepping back from the hustle-bustle of everyday life and seeking to get back to basics.

In my journey toward a simpler life, I have tried to maintain the mantra I created months ago—"Be patient, stay focused, be grateful, good things will come"—recognizing the importance of these simple words. Being patient, knowing that any current problems and complexities I am experiencing did not appear overnight, it would be unreasonable to expect them to be resolved that quickly. Staying focused, understanding the importance of remaining intent on the task at hand and cognizant of achieving the goals that have been set. Being grateful, knowing that regardless of any hardships that are being, have been, or may be encountered, there is always so much to be thankful for. I hope to never lose sight of the transformative role that gratitude plays in my life. And finally, the last verse of that mantra, trusting that if we remain patient, focused, and grateful, good things will come.

Indeed, if we slow down, delve deep, pay attention, remain mindful of our intention, stay true to our hearts' calls, and always remember to give thanks for all the abundance that surrounds us, then surely, ultimately, good things will come. A very simple recipe for life's success. Wouldn't you agree?

Wisdom

Wisdom. This word has a scientific, practical connotation as well as a more ethereal one. The term is used to describe knowledge attained through scientific facts and structured teachings. But wisdom is also gained from life experiences and innate inner knowing. When making what we hope to be sensible, wise decisions or judgments, we often rely on information received from outside sources. We also often allow our decisions to be guided by our personal experiences, including actual life events as well as an inner knowledge that for some inexplicable reason is just there, an intuition in the depths of our beings, at the foundation of the very essence of who we are.

As we age, we become more aware of the important role acquired wisdom plays in our lives. We are more in tune with the profound impact increased knowledge, this knowing, has on our day-to-day activities, thoughts, and actions. We recognize that to make wise decisions, we need to rely on information provided by outside sources as well as the guidance received from our personal compasses, our internal GPS.

If we are open to continually seeking answers to our questions and committed in our attempts to engage in and more fully understand the world around us, then we provide ourselves the opportunity to gain deeper insight into who we are as both human and spiritual beings. With this increased awareness, we can look back at our past experiences and appreciate the mistakes made and the lessons learned. We can be thankful for the fact that we are still here, and we have been given the time to evolve more fully, to strive to reach our full potentials. We can look ahead and continue moving forward with renewed vigor, hope, and faith, realizing that we have indeed grown older and wiser. We can perhaps move that much closer to achieving the wisdom so many great spiritual leaders and teachers seem to have mastered.

TRANSITIONS

The word *transition* is generally defined as a process or period of changing from one state or condition to another. As I look back and reflect on my life, it makes me wonder whether perhaps our lives can best be described as a lengthy series of transitions. Are we not continually facing new experiences and challenges that force us to adapt and evolve, requiring us to change our views, expectations, and even at times, the direction of our life courses? While some events or moments are clearly regarded as transitional, many more are quite subtle and barely recognizable. It is often not until years later, when looking back through the clear lens of a rearview mirror, that we can see them at all. The transitions we experience help us to recognize the lessons life has to offer.

In categorizing the writings for this section, I found it particularly difficult to decide whether any of them fit more clearly in this section or under "Life Lessons." While so many of the writings contained in this book have similar threads and could have been included in more than one of the sections, I found these two, "Transitions" and "Life Lessons," to be the most closely interconnected. In the end, I made a choice. I suppose it is not of any real consequence, since wherever a particular piece may have been placed, the messages relayed, the sentiments expressed all come from the same messenger on the same journey.

Running: A Metaphor for Life

For the past four decades, running has been a constant in my life. I have often described it as my drug of choice, my therapy, my equalizer. It has brought so much balance to my everyday world. It has become as vital to my daily sustenance as breathing. It is my cure-all, medicine for my soul. When tired, it awakens me. If anxious, it calms me. When confused or uncertain, it provides clarity and purpose. There is no doubt in my mind that my decision to begin running represents a key transitional moment in my life.

It was the summer of 1976. I was just completing my second year of undergraduate school and intended to register for a few courses during the summer school session. A few weeks before the registration process was to begin, I noticed that I was feeling a bit more lethargic and stressed than normal. I could not put my finger on what might be wrong, but I felt that my body was sending me a message and that I needed to pay attention.

As a typical college student, I had not been taking very good care of my body for the previous two years. I had started smoking cigarettes, lived on fast food and diet sodas, pulled many all-nighters studying for exams, and went out drinking with friends. This lifestyle was certainly not conducive to good health, and it was evident to me that my body was rebelling and that I needed to make some changes.

I decided that I would not enroll in summer school classes. Instead, I would take the time to focus on getting healthy. This would be the first time since I was a teenager that I would not be working at a summer job or going to school, so I would have no excuses if I failed to follow my commitment to seeking better health.

The first thing that I knew I had to do if I was serious about adopting a healthier lifestyle was to give up cigarettes. I cannot believe that I ever started smoking since the warnings about the harmful effects of this habit were already widely publicized. In seventh-grade science class, we were shown the disease-riddled lungs of a former smoker, an image I can still recall to this day. I was horrified at that sight and swore I would never indulge in such a habit. And yet here I was, seven years later, filling my lungs with that same carcinogen.

I realized that quitting smoking would not be easy regardless of what approach I took. I opted for the cold-turkey method rather than the gradual reduction route. While I had heard stories of people climbing the walls as part of the withdrawal process, my body's reaction was fortunately less severe. It was difficult but manageable.

It was summertime, and the weather was warm and sunny. Since I was not tied down to a work or school schedule, I decided that whenever I had a strong urge for a cigarette, I would go outside and either swim in the pool at my apartment complex or take a walk around the neighborhood. It was during this time that my relationship with running began.

I cannot say I remember the exact day I started running, but I know it was during this summer reprieve that a friend suggested that in addition to walking or swimming, perhaps running (I think we referred to it more often as jogging in those days) would be a good escape from the smoking urges. The idea of running as a leisure activity or for its basic health benefits had not yet gained mainstream popularity.

Growing up in the tropical climate of South Florida, I always spent a lot of time outdoors and participated in a variety of sporting activities, including tennis, kickball, flag football, bicycle riding, swimming, and water skiing. However, other than during required physical education classes, running was not one of those activities. I was intrigued by my friend's suggestion and figured that perhaps running would be an interesting addition to my cigarette-replacement options. I decided to put on my tennis shoes and go for a jog in the parking lot of my apartment complex.

I do not know how far or how long that initial jog was. If I had to guess, I would say probably no longer than ten minutes and no further than half a mile. I do know that there was something about it that just felt right.

I have heard that it is common for people to exchange one addiction for another, and I suppose it can be said that I replaced my smoking addiction with a running addiction. To this day, I regard it as one of the best choices I have made and am thankful for the profound impact that decision has had on my life. Running served as a cure for what was ailing me in the summer of 1976, a few months before my twentieth birthday. I have called it my drug of choice, my cure-all, every day since.

Running has been a part of my daily sustenance through many of the key transitional periods of my life, from undergraduate to law school graduation, getting married, giving birth to and raising children, practicing and retiring from the law profession, and receiving and living with a life-threatening diagnosis. Through it all, to this day, running has remained a constant. I could never have imagined what a transitional moment it would turn out to be when I made the simple, seemingly inconsequential decision to heed my friend's advice and take that first little jog around the parking lot of the apartment complex.

Over the years, I have come to view running as a metaphor for life. There are days when the wind is at our backs, pushing us along, guiding us forward, allowing us to move almost effortlessly. It is during these times that we feel at ease, strong, and invincible. And then there are times when the wind is in our faces, pushing against us, fighting our every move, challenging us to continue moving ahead. It is when we are running against the wind that we feel stressed, weak, and vulnerable. We question whether we have the stamina to keep going, to push through the adversity. Discouraged, we are often tempted to stop, to turn around, to go back, or to take the path of least resistance. It is during such times that we must slow down, remain steadfast in our efforts to plow ahead, and continue to put one foot in front of the other, trusting, knowing from previous experiences that this, too, shall pass. A knowing that we will ultimately turn the corner, and the wind will once again be at our backs, gently guiding us forward. This is how the patterns of our lives shift and sway.

Throughout it all, we must strive to find a comfortable pace, a balance that will sustain us through the ebbs and flows and help us to overcome any obstacles we confront along the way. We must realize that life is a marathon, not a sprint. We are in it for the long haul. All our training and hard work prepares us for the challenges of this long-distance run. As we persevere, as we accept the twists and turns that we encounter, our hearts become stronger; we feel more open and alive. And as we edge toward the finish line, we recognize that by staying on course, pushing through, and not giving in to all the challenges and adversities, we have learned many lessons and traveled many steps closer to reaching our ultimate destinies.

Aging

By the time I was in my mid-fifties, I had already been diagnosed with and was being treated for scleroderma. I was so grateful that the disease appeared to be under control. At the time, I was feeling good about the aging process, thankful that I was alive, and appreciating the quality of life I was fortunate to be experiencing. I had noticed some subtle changes in my appearance brought about by the natural aging process, but for the most part, I was not bothered by them.

Before my regimen of prescription medications, the dermal fibrosis had significantly reduced the range of motion in my arms. In addition, although I could still stand straight, walk, and even run, the thicker, harder skin on my legs made it difficult to bend down. If I managed to sit on the floor, it was difficult to get up gracefully.

Gradually, with the help of medication and physical therapy, my condition began to improve. The fibrosis in the arms and legs had decreased tremendously. My upper body's range of motion improved as did my lower body flexibility. I felt truly blessed as I knew that my condition could just as easily have gone in the opposite direction, requiring the use of special devices for the simple daily tasks of eating, writing, typing, and lifting, as well as necessitating the use of a wheelchair for mobility.

And so it makes sense that at the time I was not bothered by the subtle changes the natural aging process was producing—the crow's feet around the eyes, the tiny lines around the mouth. I knew that by my age, many people were undergoing or had already undergone various procedures to help camouflage the physical signs of aging. Dermatologists and plastic surgeons in South Florida are in high demand.

That brings me to today. Here I am, less than three months shy of my sixty-second birthday, and I find myself with a bit of a different perspective on this whole subject of "aging gracefully." I still believe our society places way too much emphasis on physical appearance and too often favors the youthful, unblemished look and spryness of the young over the more mature, often worn look and frailness of the elderly.

I feel we need to recognize that very real benefits come with the aging process, such as increased wisdom and a reevaluation of our priorities. It is just that I am struggling these days to accept what I consider to be the not-so-subtle evidence of my natural aging process. For the past couple years, I have found myself bothered by and focused on the increased lines, deeper wrinkles, freckles, and dark spots that seem to have appeared out of nowhere. Those years living in the

Sunshine State basking, playing, swimming, bicycling, boating, and running in the Florida sun have caught up with me.

When I was growing up in the 1950s, 1960s, and even early 1970s, we did not know about the harmful effects of the sun. My friends and I spent hours lying in the sun, smothered in baby oil, and holding a tin-foil apparatus over ourselves to attract more rays. We thought we looked healthy and beautiful and took pride in seeing who could attain the best tan. The cumulative effects of unprotected sun exposure, all those years basking and playing in the South Florida sun have taken its toll, and the visible effects have caused me to reexamine my earlier thoughts about this process of aging.

I would say that until the age of fifty-nine or sixty, I had never thought much about looking my age. If anything, I was usually seen as appearing younger than my chronological number, and it just was not an issue for me. But for the past couple of years, it seems to have become an issue. I now find myself wondering if I might appear older than I am, fearful of asking a stranger to guess my age, terrified of what his or her answer might be. Making it worse is the fact that so many of my peers have had cosmetic work done, so they look younger and fresher. That makes my dilemma more exaggerated. Part of me gets upset with myself for feeling this way, believing I am being quite superficial in my focus on physical appearance. I tell myself that I know better. Or at least thought that I knew better. I suppose I will have to accept this thought process as a normal part of aging and ultimately weigh my options and make the decisions that I believe in my heart and mind to be the ones most suitable for me.

As I grapple with these issues and the entire process of getting older, I find myself thinking about something I heard the American journalist, writer, and filmmaker Nora Ephron say in an interview several years before her death. At the time of the interview, I was probably in my late forties, perhaps just turning fifty, so I did not fully relate to her words then. But I must have somehow intuitively known that at some point, I would fully understand them because I remembered them then and certainly relate to them now. Ephron talked about how we as females are so critical of ourselves, especially of our physical appearances. When we are in our teens, twenties, and thirties, we don't like this or that about the way we look. Then when we are in our fifties and sixties, we see pictures of ourselves at those younger ages and admire how good we looked and wonder why we did not appreciate it at the time. I certainly understand the sentiment behind that now. I never liked posing for pictures and never really thought I was photogenic. But when I look back at those pictures of me in my younger years, like Ephron said, I think, *Darn, I looked good. Why didn't I recognize that more fully at the time? How I would love to look like that now.*

I suppose such is the cycle of our lives. In hindsight, it is often easy to see with the clarity of 20/20 vision. If only in our youth we possessed the wisdom that comes with age. And if only in our golden years we could get back some of the magic of our youthful innocence. I suppose the best we can do is learn to embrace every phase of our lives, live our lives to the fullest, learn and grow as we go, and accept all the ups and downs, the highs and lows each transition brings.

Aging Gracefully

Why in our Western culture do we seem so afraid of growing old? Why do we work desperately to hod on to, or recreate, the images of youth? Why do we fight so hard to turn back the hands of time, to defy the natural process of aging, to rid ourselves of the lines and wrinkles?

Surgeries, creams, injections, all kinds of processes designed to hide the signs that we are, in fact, growing older. Finding different ways of camouflaging the external images of our current stage of life. Not wanting to accept that the natural aging process has caused some withering.

What if we were to change perspective and begin to view the lines and wrinkles as symbols of a life well lived, reflections of the growth and wisdom that we have attained through the many years of living on this planet, of the many lessons learned during our time in this earth school? What if we were to allow ourselves to perceive the natural evidence of aging as telling the story of who we are, where we have been, and where our life experiences have taken us? Proud of the trials and tribulations that we have endured, struggles that we have fought through and learned from? What if we began to see the passage of time as a friend, not a foe? What if we ceased being consumed with the outer layer of ourselves and shifted attention to our internal selves, uncovering our true authenticities?

We should care for our bodies throughout the years, nourish them with good nutrition and exercise, and do our best to preserve them by treating our bodies as the temples they are designed to be. At the same time, we could stop fighting against the natural flow of time and the effects it has on our physical beings. We need to understand that this outer layer is but a mere facade behind which we sometimes choose to hide. It does not define us. It does not represent anyone's true essence. It is a limited reflection of our deepest, purest selves.

We can all recognize and appreciate the natural evolution we go through. We can learn to embrace the aging process and to allow ourselves to grow old gracefully. We must allow the light from our inner beauty to shine through and be that which is projected to ourselves and the outside world.

Back to Basics

These days, as I have taken the time to quiet down, listen, and trust my intuitive self, I have found that I seem to be returning to my most basic self, my real self, my most comfortable and spiritual self. It is as if those true parts of me that stem from childhood through adolescence and into adulthood have finally coalesced into more clarity. It is as though my true core has grown strong and sturdy. My foundation appears to have become solid, upright, and truly balanced.

I can only hope to adequately explain this process of becoming more of who I am meant to be. It is an inner knowing that the most basic parts of me—the real me—have risen to the surface. These parts of me that have always been there but have come and gone throughout the different phases of my life now seem to have lodged themselves firmly within me. They are deeply rooted. They are quite visible. I am so very aware of their presence and value in my life.

I have come to realize that the simple things matter most. It is the most basic of life's offerings that are the most valuable blessings bestowed upon us. To be able to enjoy the five senses— seeing, hearing, touching, smelling, and tasting. To be able to walk and run, to write, to move. These are grand prizes in the scheme of life, the most basic of the senses and the physical abilities that are too often taken for granted and so under appreciated.

To be united with a spouse with whom we experience life's trials and tribulations, for better or worse, for richer or poorer, in sickness and in health. To join in and follow these vows, to give true meaning to these words, is a very special gift, indeed. To be afforded the opportunity to be a parent, to truly understand what it is to love unconditionally, to know in the innermost depths of our souls that we would sacrifice it all for the sake of our children. These relationships, these most basic of all human ties and connections, are valuable treasures that give true meaning to our lives.

It is with deep appreciation and humility that I give thanks for these blessings that have been bestowed upon me. I am so very grateful for these precious resources in my life. I am truly thankful that I have somehow found my way through the complicated maze of life and to the simplest of basics.

Pivotal Choices, Difficult Decisions

F all 2000 was a key transitional period in my life. At the time, I had been practicing law for seventeen and a half years and was raising three children, ages thirteen, ten, and eight. Between the responsibilities of the law practice, the children, and the everyday household tasks, I felt as though I barely had time to breathe. My husband, Kevin, a wonderful father, and an active participant in sharing parenting and household duties, was caught up in the same whirlwind as he juggled the demands of home with the work-related issues of a general contractor running a construction company.

For a couple of years before the fall of 2000, I found myself questioning whether I could continue at this current pace. I felt that everything had become too complicated, and I yearned for a simpler life. While I had always enjoyed the type of legal work that I did, I now regarded it more and more as a burden. My interest in the work was lagging. And so the stage was set, the conditions were right, and the perfect storm was brewing. The straw that finally broke the camel's back arrived at my office door in late summer, August 2000, in the form of legal papers.

At the time, my husband had been involved for about a year and a half in a lawsuit stemming from the construction of a custom home his company completed in early 1998. The owner of the home, the individual for whom the work had been done, was a very wealthy businessman, and as we had unfortunately come to learn, someone who was quite adept at filing lawsuits and battling hard. Financially speaking, my husband and I could not compete with this multimillionaire, and he knew it.

After about eighteen months of litigation, with no settlement in sight, this man decided to add me as a party to the lawsuit. And so it was, on that summer afternoon in August, that a process server showed up at my law office and served me with the papers informing me that I was now a party in this legal proceeding. The rationale for adding me as a party was the false claim that our home renovations were paid for with funds intended to be used for the building of the claimant's home. This was untrue. Kevin and I had documentation to prove that any improvements to our home were paid for with our funds, including those obtained by taking out a second mortgage on our house. And that was the moment my back broke, the floodgates opened, and I knew that difficult choices needed to be made, choices that would result in a major transition in my life.

Now, eighteen years later, I can remember that incident and my reaction to it like it was yesterday. I had already been disturbed by the lawsuit. I did not think it was based on legitimate legal grounds, it was costly, and it added another layer of tension to our already stressful lives. But when I was served with those papers, my disturbance level rose to an entirely new dimension. I was horrified.

My initial response of feeling horrified was immediately accompanied by intense anger and utter dismay. I quickly walked back into my office, grabbed my purse and keys, and made the short ten-minute drive to my house to do the only thing I could think of in such a crazy moment— put on my running clothes and shoes and go for a run. I needed to clear my head, collect my thoughts, and figure out what on earth I was going to do and how I was going to handle this latest crisis. I knew that a run was just what the doctor ordered.

And so there I was, pounding the pavement in the sweltering heat in the mid-afternoon on a South Florida summer day. Running in the extreme heat was not unusual for me, but the thoughts rolling around in my mind were. My head was spinning, and my adrenaline was pumping as I tried to make sense of it all.

As I continued running, searching for answers to my current situation, my mind became clearer and my body calmer. Suddenly, with increased clarity and calm, came the answer I desperately needed. It was the Serenity Prayer. The words in that simple message rang loudly in my ears, reminding me of the choices I did have, urging me to regain my focus and reclaim my power. It was imperative that I accept what I could not change, change what I could, and recognize the difference between the two. In that moment, with that very powerful message reverberating through me, I knew what I had to do. While I could not alter what had already occurred as the past was beyond my control, what I did moving forward, my future, was up to me, and some important decisions needed to be made.

The first thing that I decided was that I had to make a change in my professional life. For some time, my responsibilities as an attorney had been in an increasingly uncomfortable state. Unlike my therapeutic runs, which filled me with vitality, I found that I no longer wanted to be on a fast track in my career as an attorney, continually struggling to catch my breath. I no longer wanted to live in this state of perpetual motion and constant multitasking. I also felt that I could be useful in my husband's company, helping with some behind-the-scenes legal tasks. I could do this work from home, which was an added benefit. Our children were either in or approaching adolescence, and I felt it was important for me to be at home for them. I had this strong sense that in our home life as well as my husband's business, someone needed to mind the store, and I wanted to be that someone.

As I came to realize this was the path I wanted to pursue, I knew there were two people I needed to advise of my intentions. Those two, who would be the most directly impacted by my decision, were my husband and my father. My husband, of course, because we would be losing my income from the law practice and have to rely solely on his construction company to sustain us. My husband reacted to the news as I knew he would; he provided me with his full encouragement and support. My father needed to be consulted because he was my law partner. I had been practicing with him since I passed the Florida bar in 1983. I knew he would be surprised by my decision, but he had been practicing since 1952, and my departure might give him the impetus to retire. While he was caught off guard by my decision, he understood. And as I expected, he took it as an opportunity to move forward toward the next chapter of his life.

With the support of my husband and father, I had the green light to move forward with my plan. In six months, we closed the law practice, and my father and I entered new phases of our lives.

When I decided to walk away from my law practice, many people thought my decision was quite bold and courageous. I often heard comments about how difficult it must have been for me to decide to take this action. I explained to them that this decision was an easy one. By the time I made it, what I needed to do had become so obvious to me. This was not a rash or impulsive choice. My internal GPS had been leading me in this direction for a while. I had felt for quite some time that I had lost my way, that I had somehow veered off course, and I was seeking to find my way back. It took those legal papers being handed to me on that August afternoon to provide the jolt I needed to turn me around and reroute my destination.

And now, eighteen years later, I am so thankful for that jolt and the choice it provoked me to make. The lawsuit long ago served against my husband is now nothing more than a tiny bump in the road, a barely visible speck in my rearview mirror. Still, there is no doubt about the catalytic impact this event had in leading me into new territory in my life. The decision to leave my practice gave me the opportunity to slow down, catch my breath, find my center, reassess my priorities, and reclaim my power. It provided me with the time to find that balance, that simplicity I had been so desperately seeking. Indeed, being served with court papers on that hot summer afternoon was the beginning of a new and exciting journey, one whose mission was aimed at leading me safely home.

Energy Tempered and Innocence Lost

We learn to temper our energy. We hold back, play it safe, mince our words, and refrain from showing our full emotions. We are fearful of exposing ourselves, of being hurt, of unleashing our vulnerability.

We come into this world an open book, unpretentious, filled with spontaneity, love, and wonder. Then life happens, and our experiences alter that purity. Our innocence falters. Fear and resistance set in.

We begin to see the world in a different light. The sunshine becomes a bit dimmer as gray clouds overshadow blue skies. Clarity gives way to confusion, while optimism and perseverance succumb to defeat. Our hearts often bow to our heads as our feelings give in to our thoughts. Decisions are made less from the gut as rationality pushes aside intuition.

Should it not be our mission to return to our beginnings, our true essence, that place of peace and love and calm?

Why not move toward the light? Let's embrace the divinity that lives within us. Let's surround ourselves with and give thanks for God's grace as we continue forth on our journeys. May we remain openhearted and appreciative of all that life has to offer. Let us strive to recapture the innocence with which we entered this world. Let us return to the truest and purest source of our being.

Changes

Yes! I am ready. No questions asked. No regrets. No looking back with discontentment. It is time to make this change. I must seize the moment. I am certain of this choice.

What a truly wonderful feeling. This decision is not an impulsive one. It is not the result of some sudden emotional upheaval. It has come to me slowly, in dribs and drabs, in thoughts and prayers. Now I know it is what I must do. It is the right choice.

It's funny sometimes how certain decisions seem so hard to make. We fluctuate back and forth with questions. We seek answers. We ponder so much. Then slowly, with patience, in silence, we know what it is we must do, and we just have to do it. No questions asked, no second-guessing. Our inner voices call out to us, loudly and clearly, and we must have the courage to listen, move on, and make the necessary changes.

Growth

Sitting quietly in these early evening hours, reflecting on the events of the past week. Enjoying the current tempo of life's ebb and flow. Feeling a certain tranquility within my being.

Inner peace seems to be enveloping my spirit these last few days. A sense of calm and inner serenity is ever present. I am grateful for these feelings. Thankful that I am being given the opportunity to feel this way. Knowing that this too shall pass but taking the time to appreciate this reprieve.

I am reminded of the important role solitude and stillness play in my growth process. For our spirits to develop, for our personalities to become more fully aligned with our souls, we must have quiet time to reflect and ponder. We must have time to listen more and speak less, to observe more and act less.

It is in these times of stillness that a certain inner knowing can pierce through and guide us, allowing intuition to best serve us. It is a gradual process, this period of becoming true to our hearts' calls. Over time, we realize that inner listening helps us to reform and transform our views and functions in our day-to-day experience. When we are open, we can receive direction. Our spirits can continue to seek and grow, to reap and sow. It is then we recognize that we are growing firmer, simpler, quieter, warmer.

Reaping and Sowing

I t is often said that there are times when we reap and times in which we sow. Sometimes it is difficult to differentiate between the two.

I am not quite sure what to call this period for me. In some ways, I am reaping the benefits of so many years of searching, reflecting, reading, listening, wondering. In other ways, I am sowing now, embarking on new connections and activities filled with additional questions and thoughts.

Perhaps they are not meant to be entirely separate processes. Maybe there is a continual blending of the two. If you think about it, are we not constantly reaping and sowing as we continue moving forward on our life journeys? Aren't our lives constant arrays of changing patterns? Events come and go. The years move on, and time seems to speed up as we grow older.

Perhaps the answer is not to attempt to identify the reaping and sowing. Rather, to continue to trust that the world is moving forward as it must and that our places within it are as it is supposed to be. Continue to impart your footprints on this canvas of life. Remain steadfast in your values and convictions. Continue to listen to your heart's call, and follow the road you have been traveling on, the one that you know is the right path for you.

There will be times when your sense of direction will be tested. Events and people will present some obstacles along the way, and you may be inclined to be steered off course. It is during such times that you must continue to have faith that you are headed in the right direction. Do not diverge from the path you know is the right one for you. Trust what you know to be true down to the innermost depths of your being. Let that inner compass be your guide.

Perhaps we can continue on our current courses, reaping the benefits of what we have sown while at the same time, sowing new seeds that will blossom with the lessons of tomorrow.

The Shift

There are certain times when shifts take place in our lives. Sometimes we are aware of the precise moment such a shift happens. Other times, we realize that one has occurred, but exactly when and where, we are unclear.

Interestingly, these shifts that show up in our day-to-day existence are often so unexpected and unplanned. They make their ways into all facets of our lives. Sometimes we are baffled by their presence, uncertain of their purposes and reasons for their appearances at a particular time. If open, we embrace them and allow them to help guide us on our journeys. We accept them as necessary parts of our evolution in the here and now.

An example of a shift in my life that was described in detail previously was my decision to leave my law practice. This was a major shift that crystallized on the day I was served with court papers. But the shift had been developing gradually over many months. The day I was served merely provided the impetus to make this life-altering change.

Another, more subtle example of a shift in my life, which was also discussed previously, was the day I took Oprah's advice and read Sarah Ban Breathnach's book *Simple Abundance*. That book helped me to realize the important role gratitude plays in our everyday lives. The author's emphasis on approaching life with a mindset of abundance rather than lack provided me with a profound shift in the way I began to view the people and events in my life. I found myself being grateful for the simplest of life's pleasures. Writing in my daily gratitude journal became an essential part of my everyday routine and transformed the way I began to recognize the extraordinary in what is often regarded as merely ordinary.

We understand that these shifts—whether subtle or clear—are indeed integral to our life plans, the master design that has been so precisely formulated before we arrived at this earth school. We should not challenge these shifts. We should allow ourselves to flow gently with their force. We must trust that they are vital to our growth processes and that they are leading us in the right direction and will help to carry us to our ultimate destinies.

LIFE LESSONS

The seeking, questioning, thoughts, feelings, and experiences revealed in the pages of this book were born out of my desire to find answers and my quest to understand the world around me and my place within it. In my search, as I traveled further and dug deeper, I gained insight and learned many important lessons.

I came to appreciate the vital role Mother Nature plays in my life and how much all of us can learn from recognizing the similarities between her patterns and the ebbs and flows of our lives. I grew in my understanding of the strong shared desire we have to feel connected to each other and to the world in which we live, to recognize our commonalities, to believe that what we say and do matters, and to love and be loved. I discovered that there is so much in this universe that defies explanation—the seemingly inherent perfection of the natural world, events that occur, people who enter our lives, our very existence as the complex beings that we are—all of it somehow, on some level, so masterfully designed, hinting at some divine, otherworldly power.

I have become more aware of the importance of remaining true to myself, of not compromising my values, of trusting and listening to my heart's call. In the process, I grew more cognizant of my moral compass, my internal GPS, and the necessity of allowing it to be my most trusted guide. I found there are certain situations, events, or people that prompt us to make decisions or take actions that result in pivotal shifts in our lives. Sometimes they are quite evident and can be seen with great clarity. Other times, they are more subtle and perhaps remain unrecognized for a while. How critical these encounters are! How amazing it is when we make the connections!

My seemingly endless search is to discover more about myself and the world around me. Everything I am learning is part of my growth process and an expression of my journey. Each lesson has propelled me to where I am and who I am today. Every hard-fought decision and every disappointment, every roadblock and every setback, even every uninvited emotional storm brings the gift of special life lessons wrapped in an unexpected package. I am grateful for every lesson. I am grateful for this bountiful search.

Adversity

Adversity. I believe it brings out the best and the worst in us. It is through adversity that we are forced to dig deep into the innermost depths of our beings. It is during turbulent times that we find ourselves doing more pondering, examining, and probing. We long for answers to some of life's questions: "Why is this happening to me?" "What am I supposed to learn from this experience?" "What gifts is this experience of adversity laying at my feet?"

During difficult periods, we tend to reflect more, listen more intently, and yearn for truth and meaning. We wonder whether our faith or integrity will falter. We question whether we can, in fact, endure.

As we struggle to stay afloat, as we search for answers to our dilemmas, we often discover facets of ourselves that we did not know existed. Perhaps we find that we are stronger than we thought we were as we muster the strength to keep moving forward despite the seemingly insurmountable efforts to bring us down. Perhaps we learn that although it might be tempting, we will not allow ourselves to stoop to the level of our opponents or give in to and become the negativity surrounding us.

It is during periods of adversity that we can connect most deeply to our internal compasses. An inner voice calls out to us, reminding us that we have survived hostile and adverse conditions before, and just like then, this too shall pass. It encourages us to stay the course and provides us with the hope and courage needed to do so. This voice of encouragement manages to overshadow the uncertainty and confusion as it permeates us. It diffuses the doubt as we trust its message, recognizing it to be a force far greater and more powerful than our present circumstances. It can perhaps best be described as our authentic selves shining through, guiding us along, pushing us forward, and reminding us to trust that out of the adversity and hardship will come true knowledge, personal growth, and ultimate joy.

Curveballs

As we age and look back and reflect on the stories of our lives, we begin to recognize a pattern of ebb and flow, ups and downs, highs and lows. We come to realize that life as we know it in this earth school is ever changing. It is not static. It does not stand idle. It is continually evolving, and we, as key players, are constantly transitioning with it.

Just when we think we have reached a point of calm and understanding, when we believe that we have figured out the answer to some of life's key questions, when we feel a certain sense of inner peace and wisdom, a curveball is often thrown our way. Suddenly, we find ourselves feeling confused and uncertain. We are left thinking that perhaps we are no further along than when we started, the same as when we began, a novice still. These curveballs seem to appear out of nowhere, pitched to us by some unknown random player, one who is attempting to catch us off guard. When such pitches come toward us, we must maintain our composure, plant our feet firmly on the ground, dig in our heels, and rely on the strength built from the successes we have had on previous trips to the plate.

We need to be resolute in our determination not to allow these curveballs to compromise the confidence and knowledge we have gained through the many years of playing this sport. We must stand tall, align ourselves with home base, and remain focused and committed, keeping in mind the fact that we have seen these types of wild pitches before, and we were able to overcome such adversarial encounters in the past. We must remember that this is not our first time at bat. And drawing on prior experiences, we need to trust that with persistent effort and resolve, we will be able to move beyond this formidable challenge.

Recognize that this is merely one more obstacle coming at us from the mound, one that, although similar, is not quite the same as the previous distractions that stood in our way. We must believe that while our initial swings may result in some strikes and foul balls, if we continue to pay attention, remain in the zone, and keep swinging, we will ultimately be able to make the right contact. We will get that hit. It may come in the form of a single or double or triple. It may be an infield or outfield drive. It may veer to the right or the left or stay center. However, neither the direction nor distance are what matters. The fact that we made the connection is what counts, a reminder that perseverance and hard work have paid off. We are reaping the benefits of our numerous hours of training, all the practice and play of the past. It has fostered and nurtured our talents, provided us the opportunities to improve our skills, and prepared us to face this current opposition. It has spawned within us a certain confidence to trust our innate abilities, a yearning to strive for and believe that we can reach our full potentials. We realize that the refusal to quit, instead choosing to keep on swinging, has brought us that much closer to achieving our goals.

By remaining steadfast, by staying on track and sticking to the plan, by refusing to allow the difficulties to deter us, we have perhaps moved ever closer to—and set the stage for—showcasing the full range of our athletic prowess, our very special gifts. Just maybe we will hit the big one, knock the ball out of the park, perhaps a grand slam. Or better yet, end the game with the ultimate achievement, a walk-off home run. At the end of the day, when all is said and done, is it not, after all, just another day at the park, complete with one more curveball to challenge us, to test our resolve in this complex game called life?

Daring the Unconventional

Call me crazy, but I have been known to do some impromptu things. As much as I am not an impulsive person, I am also in many ways a bit unconventional, and thus, I am sometimes inclined to go against the grain, to defy the norm, to march to the beat of my own drummer.

While by nature I would not regard myself as a risk-taker, there have been times when I have been quite daring, when I have stepped out of the box and been willing to allow my heart to guide me in directions and down paths that perhaps my head would avoid.

Looking back, I see a pattern of fitting into society's norms while at the same time, remaining in many ways on the cutting edge. A certain dichotomy seems to flow through my being, defining the very essence of who I am. I suppose this is representative of the yin and yang that exists in all our lives. We humans are complex beings. There is no cookie-cutter mold to define us. It is important to recognize and accept the contradictions and differences within oneself and those around us, and as individuals, to continue moving toward our unique authenticities, always seeking to become all that we are destined to be.

Expectations

We experience many times in our lives when our expectations are not met. We are left feeling disappointed and disillusioned that something has not worked out quite the way we hoped it would or that someone has not responded or reciprocated in the manner we anticipated. We thought a scenario would look one way, but it ended up appearing quite different.

What causes us to have these expectations? Why do we expect a certain response? Why do we envision results that perhaps are not reasonable? And how do we respond to these unmet expectations? Do we draw inward? Do we lose faith? Do we become cynical, fearful, or resistant? Or do we seek to find lessons in these unmet expectations? Do we take these disappointments—no matter how great or how small—and learn from them, striving to gain understanding and wisdom from their presence in our lives? Do they create in us a desire to examine our actions and reactions to others and help us to be more accepting, patient, humble, and kind?

As is true with so many of our life experiences, how we view our unmet expectations, and the perspectives we choose, will influence how we continue to evolve on our journeys. The choice is ours. Let us not waste any opportunity to grow into our best, brightest, most authentic selves.

Life's Dance

Life is the dancer and you are the dance.

—Eckhart Tolle

Walking along a dirt road this morning, amid the backdrop of the Blue Ridge Mountains, soaking in the beauty of these natural surroundings. Thoughts and feelings flow in and out like breath. Pondering the similarities between our human lives and those of all living things with whom we share this planet. Each part of a wonderful dance.

A combination of so many different moves and conditions. At times gliding along, almost effortlessly, appearing to be in perfect rhythm with life's flow—like the wild horse running gracefully through the pasture, or the ballerina floating across the stage. Times when it feels like a soft, gentle breeze is guiding us steadily forward.

And then suddenly, without warning, the winds pick up. The strong gusts appear, forcing us to hasten the pace challenging us to maintain our balance. We realize we are amid a fast dance, one that has a rock-and-roll type of feel. Like the squirrel scurrying feverishly toward the tree where it hopes it can climb to safety, or the deer whose carefree, easy gait shifts into a more rapid, frenetic gear as it tries to reach the dense brush where it can hide, sometimes we find ourselves frantically searching for a haven. We look for shelter from the storm that seems to be brewing. We seek answers, wanting to understand the twists and turns, wondering how it all could have changed so quickly.

How could the dance have transformed almost instantly from the grace and ease of the ballet to the brash and tumultuous rock-and-roll? Why, when we thought that perhaps we were finally in sync, moving in harmony with the music, do we find ourselves struggling to remain on our feet, trying desperately not to lose our footing? How do we refrain from giving in to these strong forces, from not giving up and allowing ourselves to fall?

As we continue our searches for responses to these questions, delving further into finding the meaning behind it all, we are once again reminded of the impermanent nature of such inquiries. Have we not yet learned that our lives, just like all of nature, are ever changing? That even as we formulate our questions, both the question and the answer need revision? Such is the essential dilemma of the dance.

As part of God's magnificent creations, we must continue moving forward, placing one foot in front of the other, accepting that we will slip and stumble along the way. As we edge across the dance floor, we must trust that the moves we make, both subtle and bold, and the steps we take, both large and small, are being guided by God's grace, and with that all-powerful force behind us, we know that we will be able to master what has been choreographed specifically for us in this place, at this time. Our very own solo performances, our life's dances.

Our Mission

It has been a long time since I have written. Although growth and inner searching have continued, the written expression has been idle, lying dormant for a while. I am not quite sure what I am feeling these days. A certain tranquility and sense of peace, but at the same time, a certain restlessness and confusion. These contrasting emotions, this tug-of-war within, cause me to question the very essence of my life's purpose and at times elusive mission.

Life is strange. The events, the people who find their way along our paths, the doors that open, and those that close. The feelings that are stirred, the heartfelt expressions of love and gratitude that seem to flow. An inner knowing that seems to guide us if we stay open to receiving the signals along the way. An acceptance and sense of grace that transcends it all if our hearts remain open to the natural ebb and flow of life.

Ultimately, I believe we are spiritual beings having a human experience, and in our humanness, we are destined to encounter many challenges on our life journeys. Perhaps our mission here is to face the challenges head-on, learn from them, and use the lessons taught to grow into wiser and more compassionate beings. And as we continue to evolve, we must remember the importance of seeking the light and moving away from the darkness. We must allow the outstretched arms of God's grace to embrace us in their all-loving and powerful grasp to hold us tight, to love us deeply. Perhaps then we will be able to say our missions have been accomplished.

Our Paths

I believe we come into this world with a predetermined plan for our lives, a set path to follow, one that has been mapped out specifically for us, a route only we are destined to travel. As we embark on our journeys, we are given certain tools and some necessities that will help to guide us and keep us safe along the way. These appear in different forms, in varying degrees, from natural talents and personal attributes to inherent values and innate knowing. It is these forces that seem to serve as our inner compasses, propelling us forward and keeping us moving in the right direction.

They are there when we come to a fork in the road, speaking to us, instructing us on which way to veer. Sometimes the instructions come in the form of a whisper and other times, as a booming, boisterous voice. But regardless of the tone, these cues act as an internal GPS that tells us which way to turn, prompting us to stay on track and allowing us to remain on the path toward our preset destinations.

As we continue roaming, remaining steadfast in the desire to reach our goals, we are confronted by various terrains. From rugged and rocky to flat and smooth. From rain-soaked and ice-covered to dry and slip-free. On uphill climbs, where we struggle to catch our breath and find ourselves feeling almost powerless, we fight to muster the strength to continue, to not turn back, not quit in midstream, only to transition to downhill glides, where we are inhaling and exhaling effortlessly, believing ourselves invincible as our calm, graceful strides carry us forward.

The key, we come to realize as we traipse through these different landscapes, is to accept that all of it—the twists and turns, the ups and downs, the rough, the ragged, the clear—is a natural and necessary part of our life's obstacle courses, one that is unique to us. No two individuals have been carved an identical pathway.

We will meet fellow travelers along the way. Some will be just passersby, perhaps moving in the opposite direction, to whom we will simply smile and wave. Others will engage us in conversation, brief dialogue, perhaps become acquaintances with whom we shall spend a limited amount of time before parting ways. Then there will be those with whom we will develop much deeper bonds. The ones who will accompany us for long periods on our journeys, who will walk beside us. Those with whom we shall share many meaningful experiences and feel comfortable expressing some of our deepest vulnerabilities. As we navigate through uncertain and unchartered territories, these very special comrades, our most beloved sojourners, shall help to provide us with the stamina to stay the course, give us the strength to keep pushing ahead, and the impetus to not waiver in our determination to continue. They are the angels God, the divine creator of this magnificent adventure, has placed in our midst so we may fully appreciate the spectacular nature of this guided tour laid out just for us. Our very own original life path.

Park Bench Reflections

I am sitting quietly on the bench at the neighborhood park, watching people as they pass by. Some are running swiftly, others strolling calmly, some by themselves, others with a companion or two. Different ages, genders, body types, and ethnicities. Some looking pensive, deep in thought. Others appearing carefree, playful, filled with laughter and joy. I pause for a moment to think about how these passersby represent aspects of ourselves, of our lives, of the many phases we go through in this lifetime. The ups and downs, the serious, the difficult, the mundane, the happy, the extraordinary.

Silently observing these strangers seems to stir something deep within, creating a feeling of thoughtfulness and reflection, setting a movie reel in motion, a video of many experiences encountered thus far. Rewinding the recording to start at the beginning, to trace the footsteps taken on the path to date. I want to view all that has been captured in chronological order from early childhood until today.

Moving slowly through the film, not wanting to bypass any key moments, hitting the pause button frequently along the way, freezing the frame to focus on the people and places, the thoughts and feelings associated with their presence, and trying to fully understand their significance in this magnificent production.

As we review these snapshots of our journeys, as we open the floodgates into our lives, memories and emotions come pouring in. We find ourselves wondering what editing we would do if provided the opportunity to do so. What scenes would we choose to erase? Which ones would we want to replay? After all, it is a natural human desire to want to make some changes.

Yet as the reel of tape concludes as there are no more past experiences to recall, we realize that we cannot alter the events that have already been recorded, moments that have come and gone, those that have been etched in our individual histories, in the scrapbooks of our minds. What we can do is recognize that as older and wiser directors of this creative pursuit, we can take the many valuable lessons that we have learned from our previous recordings, hit the play button, and fill the screen with new nostalgia and scenarios, doing our best not to repeat outdated and ill-advised scenes from the past.

We need to resume filming with the knowledge that this documentary is continuing to evolve, and how it will end remains a mystery. The outcome is still untold. It is a personal and highly individualized work in progress, a true original, not a remake of an old flick. We must accept that while this may never be regarded as a perfect production, it is an important artistic masterpiece that we need to continue to pursue. And we must have faith that, if we adjust the settings properly and pay close attention to the details, we can, with the sharp eye of the camera lens, zoom in and focus with precision. Sitting on a park bench with just the right amount of light, perhaps we can create that unique and authentic story, the grand story of our lives.

Perception

have heard it said that there is no reality, only perception. I find this to be a very interesting concept. Perception explains why one person sees the glass as half empty and another individual sees the same glass as half full. It is the same glass, the identical physical object, but the perception of it is viewed so differently.

We have people who are described as optimists and others who are labeled pessimists. This is the reason that some with such a seemingly small lot in life can maintain positive and hopeful outlooks while some who appear to have it all project auras of negativity and hopelessness. Some have riches and see rags, and some who have but mere rags and see such beautiful, wonderful riches.

Perception is such a powerful factor in determining how we see the world. It is vital to our overall outlook and appreciation of life. If only my perception may be one of seeing beauty and wonder and joy, then my reality shall be so beautiful and wonderful and joyous. If only my perception shall be one of seeking to find the sacred in the ordinary and abundance where others may see lack, then my reality, my life, shall be fruitful and wondrous and worthy of having been.

Reflections

I am sitting quietly this morning, taking a few moments to reflect and ponder. Feeling a sense of calm, a peaceful balance, and a natural inner flow these past few days. Believing that I am experiencing some of the results of following the mantra I created for myself approximately eighteen months ago: to be patient, stay focused, remain grateful, and trust that good things will come.

Life is indeed a journey. I truly believe we are put on this earthly plane to grow, to become more conscious and evolved beings. The struggles are many. The challenges are often painful and disconcerting. Yet I think it is a destiny that we have chosen, one that we mapped out with great precision before we arrived in this human form.

It is not meant to be easy. It is not possible to be perfect. It is imperative that there be loss and heartache along the way. But it is as it is supposed to be. All that we encounter—each relationship, each situation—is a necessary part of the master plan we set for ourselves. There are no coincidences. There is no good or bad luck. It is as it must be. It is a puzzle, each piece a necessary part to complete the whole.

If only I may continue to grow firmer, simpler, quieter, warmer. If only I may continue to stay focused, be patient, and be grateful. If only I may continue to strive to be the best that I can be, to become all that I am supposed to be. If only I may continue to be impeccable with my word, to live within the bounds of my integrity, to be nonjudgmental, to set ego aside, and to allow humility, love, and kindness to be my guide. If only I may allow my internal compass to remain steady, to flow smoothly, to be a barometer of peace and calm, no matter how much turmoil and adversity surrounds me. If only I may instill in my children, who I consider to be the most precious gifts that have been bestowed upon me, the importance of these qualities in one's life. Perhaps then, my mission for this life will be fulfilled. Perhaps then, on my departure, this world will be a bit better for my having been here. Although in a small or seemingly inconsequential way, a little better, nonetheless.

Something More

What is this deep longing running so powerfully throughout my being? Such a strong pull tugging at the innermost depths of my soul. A powerful force making its presence known in the deepest core of me. Recognizing this feeling as coming from an energy source far greater than my everyday perception of reality, I want to describe it as a yearning for something more.

I feel so deeply sometimes. It is as though all barriers are removed. An energy of love and understanding is so ever present. What is this that seems to recur in patterns throughout my life? What is the message? What is the purpose? Where will this energy take me in my life? Will these questions ever be answered here on this earthly plane? Will this sense of longing, this deep desire for something more, ever be fulfilled? Is it a mere dream that will never become a reality? Or is it my destiny, leading me slowly down a path to be revealed when the time is right? I am often left with a burning desire to receive answers to these questions.

I must continue moving forward on my journey with faith and courage, trusting that life is unfolding as it should and that all situations are necessary to my growth process. I shall accept this deep longing, this powerful pull, as an integral part of me. I will continue to believe that all is as it is meant to be, as it needs to be. I trust that my heart will lead me in the right direction. It will take me where I need to be. I must surrender my endless questioning and allow the deep inner knowing to surface. I must accept my life, this life, at this moment in time. I must remember the serenity prayer to "accept the things I cannot change, the courage to change the things I can, and the wisdom to know the difference."

Release Me: A Prayer

Release me from the shackles of the constricting thoughts in my head, and deliver me, let me live in the free-flowing spirit of my heart.

Let my heart be the compass that guides me, the vessel that helps me to navigate the ever-changing currents of my life. Let it be what steers me in the right direction. What leads me back when I have unwittingly veered off course. May my heart be the trusted GPS to which I turn when I am not quite sure which path to follow, which route to take, and what avenue to pursue. Let me allow it to be my most trusted companion, my tried-and-true adviser, my confidante. Let me learn to listen to what is often its quiet, subtle voice, to heed its soft nudge, to pay attention to its gentle whispers.

Provide me the courage to remain faithful to this source, to recognize and appreciate the importance of its presence in my life. Allow me quiet moments of reflection so that I may tap into the full breadth of knowledge that this very special teacher can provide, the wide array of lessons to be taught.

As I continue moving forward on this life journey, let me seek to bask in the sweet melodic flow of the rhythm of my heart. Let it be what allows me to break free of the too-often cumbersome constrictions of the thoughts roaming in my head. Please release me from the shackles of my mind, and let me live in the free-flowing spirit of my heart.

The Test

This is a test. For the next four years, you will endure an enormous amount of stress. Your mission is to stay focused on the tasks at hand, hold your head high, and grow in wisdom and strength as a result of having survived the challenge. Your survival throughout this mission will depend on your ability to maintain your faith, dig to the very core of your being, never compromise your integrity, and trust that if you remain focused, patient, and grateful, good things will come.

Your reward, should you survive this mission, is that you will emerge a stronger, kinder, wiser, and more compassionate and enlightened human being. The numerous hours of soul-searching this experience will force on you, the many questions raised about the meaning of your life and the circumstances within it will enable you to discover your authenticity. You will become more fully acquainted with your true and most loving self as your personality becomes more fully aligned with your soul.

There will be times throughout this experience when you will question if you have the strength to carry on. You will silently wonder whether there is any light at the end of what appears to be this very dark tunnel. There will be many moments when you feel discouraged as you seem to be taking two steps backward for each step forward, and you may be inclined to give up or back down. At precisely such moments, it is imperative that you reach deep down, and with quiet determination and resolve, continue moving ahead slowly and steadily.

If you remain steadfast in your refusal to quit, defiant against the efforts to defeat you, and resolute in the mindset that failure is not an option, you *will* reach the end of this mission feeling emboldened by your perseverance and resolve. You will realize that you have completed and passed the test. You will be able to pause and take time to reflect on and appreciate the many lessons learned along the way, all while knowing that there will be many more lessons to learn and many more tests to take.

THE UNEXPECTED

I spent most of the summer months of 2017 and 2018 in my father's North Carolina mountain home. It was during those summer months, in the peace and tranquility of that environment, that I worked on compiling the writings that appear on these pages. When I left my mountain retreat to return to South Florida in late August 2018, I believed my writings were complete and that my next step was to begin putting the raw material into proper book form. In other words, I had to explore the publishing process, which I knew absolutely nothing about. What I did not know at that time, and what I could not have anticipated, was that for the next six months, events would occur that would challenge everything I thought I had learned in life. These events would lead me to the realization that my story was not complete. It would soon become clear to me that there was one very important chapter that needed to be written before I could call my manuscript complete.

On January 19, 2019, I suffered a hemorrhagic stroke and was transported by ambulance to the emergency room of Memorial Regional Hospital. On the short ride to the hospital, the EMTs were in communication with the emergency room staff. Based on my symptoms, it was believed that I had suffered a stroke. When the ambulance arrived at the hospital, I was immediately taken to the adult stroke unit and put into a CT scanner, where a brain scan was performed. While I was foggy-headed and my thought processes and reactions were clearly slower than normal, I remained conscious during this entire process. Within a few minutes, the emergency room neurologist poked his head into the machine. He told me that I had a brain bleed, the next seventy-two hours were critical, and I would be monitored closely during that time to determine whether I would require surgery or any other intervention. He also asked if I had ever had a seizure, to which I replied that I had not. I remember wondering whether I should tell him that I had a younger sister who had been diagnosed with epilepsy at six months of age and experienced seizures from that time until her death at thirteen months old, when she died in her sleep from a seizure.

Though I decided not to mention my sister's history of seizures to the doctor, I was struck by the scary thought that perhaps now, with the bleeding going on in my brain, the trauma of a seizure disorder could be coming back to haunt me.

A few hours after the scan and a brief interaction with the neurologist, I was taken from the emergency room to the intensive care unit (ICU), where I remained for the next three days. During that time, I was hooked up to machines that constantly monitored my blood pressure, heart rate, and respiration. My finger was poked every few hours to make sure that my blood sugar (glucose) levels were under control. I think that once a day, blood was drawn from my arm to check the status of my body's overall functioning. In those three days, I also underwent two more CT scans, a two-hour MRI and MRA, an angiogram, an EKG, and an EEG. My recollection of those first few days is quite hazy as I drifted in and out of consciousness. I remember my loving family being by my side through all of it, and I was, and still am, so thankful for that.

The good news is that the updated CT scans showed that the bleeding had stopped, and it was determined that I would not require surgical intervention. At the end of seventy-two hours, I was moved from the ICU to a room in the neurology unit, where I remained for the next couple of days. During this time, I was poked and prodded a bit less and was a little more aware of my surroundings and the people who were coming in and out.

By this time, I had become fully cognizant of the fact that my left side was paralyzed. I could not move my fingers, arms, hands, toes, feet, or legs. I referred to my left side as being "dead," but the medical term for it is flaccid or hemiplegic. I had sensations in these areas, so I could feel if someone or something touched my extremities, but I could not move any of those parts of my body. It was explained to me that the hemorrhagic stroke I had suffered was a bleed on the right side of my brain, which affects the left side of the body. It also affects spatial awareness, and I had what was referred to as "left neglect," which meant that I was not fully aware of the left side of my surroundings. This was evident when I was asked to draw a clock and I drew a circle with the numbers twelve through six on the right half of the clock, leaving the left half of the clock completely blank. I also kept looking to my right and had to be reminded to turn my head to the left to look at people or things that were positioned on that side.

While I was in the neurology unit, they sent a physical therapist to help me attempt to walk. And with the aid of a walker, the therapist on one side, and a nurse on my other side, I was able to drag my body a short distance. Suddenly, the ability to walk, to put one foot in front of the other, had become a nearly impossible task.

Five days after my stroke, I was transported from Memorial Regional Hospital to Memorial Rehabilitation Institute. This would be my home for the next three weeks. It was on this ride to the rehabilitation center that the reality of my current situation began to sink in. It hit me hard. As I lay helplessly on the stretcher, I was transported along a route that was very familiar to me. One I had driven so many times during the fourteen years I had been living in Hollywood, passing the stores and other local places I frequented regularly. All I could think of was the fact that my life would never be the same. I wondered if I would ever be able to drive myself down these roads or walk into any of these places again.

As these thoughts ran through my mind, my eyes filled with tears, and the floodgates opened. There had been some crying episodes in the preceding five days since the stroke, but somehow, this time was different. This was completely uncontrollable. I think that for the first time, I was becoming acutely aware of the magnitude of the challenge confronting me. I realized that all the lessons I had learned thus far, the experiences I had encountered, all I had come to hold as my truths, and all that I had written about were now being tested in a very dramatic way. I was going to be forced to dig deep and search deep to navigate my way through and survive. I also came to the realization that the written material for this book, which I thought had been completed the previous summer, was not quite finished. I knew there was now going to be a new and most unexpected chapter to write.

Something else that I remember so vividly about my fateful ambulance ride was the kindness and compassion of the two men who transported me. I was embarrassed that I was crying in front of these two strangers. But as I attempted to apologize for my tears, they offered me words of encouragement and prayer. One of the men showed me a large scar on his head, the result of a terrible car accident he was involved in several years ago. He told me that he had gone through a long recovery process and offered me hope that my recovery would go well. I also remember thinking that I did not want these men, or any of the other strangers who saw me crying on the gurney to think I was crying because I was feeling sorry for myself. After all, years before this experience, I had come to believe that when facing hardship, one should not ask, "Why me?" but, "Why not me?" I wanted to tell them I was not crying out of self-pity. Rather, I was aware enough to know that we all encounter hardships in this broken world, and I believed this was all part of God's master plan for my life, and I would have to accept the obstacles placed in my path. I wanted to let them know that I was grateful the stroke had not attacked the left side of my brain and because of that, my speech and memory were intact. I still had full use of my right side, which was my dominant side. I wanted to express all these thoughts that were racing through my mind, but the tears were flowing too forcefully, preventing me from uttering the words.

The tears were still pouring out of me when I was wheeled into my room and was greeted by the nurse and patient care assistant. They were both friendly and cheerful as they welcomed me to my new temporary abode and offered sincere words of encouragement. I would come to know them quite well as each would be on staff several times during my three-week inpatient stay. I would also have an opportunity to visit them after my discharge, when I returned to the facility for outpatient therapy. The nurse, whose name was Oana, has reminded me on several occasions of how I tearfully answered her questions during my initial evaluation. The evaluation involved squeezing her fingers with my hands and moving my feet and toes up and down. The strength and mobility on my right side were pretty good, but when it came to movement on the left, as Oana would later remind me, my response through tears was, "I can do nothing." Oana also happened to be my nurse the day after I regained the ability to move my toes, which was a little less than two weeks after that initial evaluation. I could swear from the big smile on her face and the bear hug she gave me that she was as happy for me as I was for myself.

My emotions during my stay at the rehabilitation center fluctuated immensely, ranging from joy and laughter to tears and sadness. Perhaps the clearest example of this occurred during my first weekend there. The schedule at the rehab center consisted of a minimum of three hours a day of therapy Monday through Friday. On weekends, it was one day on and one day off. Since I had arrived late in the day on Thursday, my first therapy session began the next day, Friday. I worked hard that first day, and it was immediately evident to me that this was going to be a difficult process.

The big goal I accomplished in my first physical therapy session was "walking" approximately thirty feet while holding onto a stationary bar on one side and my therapist on the other, helping to push me along. It was hard to believe that less than a week and a half earlier, I was able to run three miles effortlessly. Walking thirty feet on my own had become an impossible task. During that session, one of my sons and a friend of his, whom I knew well, walked in, and as they saw me struggling to walk, I broke down in tears. All I could think of in that moment was how I had gone from the "running mom" to the "cannot-even-walk mom." I was able to stop the tears, regain my composure, complete the session, and was wheeled back to my room in the wheelchair, which was quickly becoming my primary mode of transportation. Because of the paralysis on my left side, I was not even able to navigate the wheelchair on my own. I was quickly learning that even a wheelchair can be difficult to use properly when one side of your body is not working.

Later that evening, several friends and family members were visiting me, and I was in surprisingly good spirits. I was joking around and was more talkative than usual. At one point, I needed to use the bathroom, which was in my room. As my husband was wheeling me into the bathroom, my guests were still laughing over something funny I had said. I looked back at them and jokingly commented that perhaps I was finding a new calling—stand-up comedian. My daughter, who can always be counted on for a quick retort, immediately responded, "I do not think stand-up is the correct word at this time," to which I replied, "You're right. I guess a better way to describe my new calling would be wheelchair comedian." We all broke out in even more laughter. A nurse who happened to be walking by came into the room and commented how unusual it was to see so many smiling faces and hear so much laughter under these circumstances. The tears shed earlier in the day felt like a distant memory. Little did I know that this was merely a reprieve, and the emotional tides would shift once again tomorrow.

The next morning, I woke up feeling good about the fun we had the night before. I was eager to attend the cooking class, which as part of recreational therapy, was the only therapy on my schedule for that day. I was wheeled into the room where the class was to take place. A portion of the room was set up as a kitchen. When I arrived, five other patients were sitting at the table; the six of us would be the ones taking that day's ninety-minute class. There was also a recreational therapist, an occupational therapist, a recreational therapy student, and a high school student volunteer. It immediately became apparent that I was the only newcomer to the group and the most physically challenged. I was the only one for whom one side of the body was not working. After a few minutes of introductions, we were given latex-type hospital gloves. Because of the paralysis of my left hand and arm, and the fact that my left hand was stuck in a clenched-fist position and barely able to open at all, I was incapable of putting the gloves on by myself. Noticing my inability, the recreational therapist, Kristie, came over and put them on for me. This is another example of the kindness and compassion offered by hospital staff.

Next, we were each given a copy of two recipes listing the ingredients and preparation instructions for the two items we would be cooking. We were asked to choose which preparatory task we wanted to have assigned to us. Because of my limitations, there was very little that I could do, so my task was chosen for me. My assignment was to chop walnuts. Using my right hand, I picked up the shelled walnut pieces, placed them in a plastic Ziploc bag, and began feverishly pounding them with a tool. While others used knives to slice and dice vegetables, and another stood at the stove sautéing the vegetables that had been sliced, I sat chopping walnuts with the one hand that was still useable. As I pounded those walnuts and watched the others slicing and dicing and standing up and cooking, the reality of my current situation hit me hard. I was reminded of the significant challenges that I was facing and was overcome with feelings of helplessness and hopelessness. In that moment, the tears began flowing, and the floodgates opened once again.

This time it was the occupational therapist, Jillian, who came to my rescue. She asked me if I would like to leave the room and go out into the hallway to talk. Through my tears, and now very runny nose, I nodded, so she grabbed a box of tissues and wheeled me away from the table and into the hallway, where we stayed for the remaining twenty minutes of the class. Jillian spent time talking with me, asking me questions about myself, attempting to gain some insight into who I was and why participation in the class had made me so upset. As I struggled to speak through the tears, I told her that I was realizing how disabled I now was. I explained how, since the age of twenty, I had run three to five miles a day, and now, after forty-two years of that, I could not even stand up and step out of the wheelchair. I could not put on my gloves. I could not slice and dice vegetables or stand and cook at the stove. As she handed me tissue after tissue, she told me that I reminded her of another patient she had worked with a few years prior, and that patient now volunteered as a mentor. She asked if she could invite that mentor to visit me. She mentioned that this patient, now mentor, had also been a runner before the brain injury that had, like me, caused her to be paralyzed on her left side.

Although the time spent talking to Jillian had helped me regain some control of my emotions, the tears were still flowing as I was wheeled back to my room on the sixth floor. I do not think I thanked Jillian at the time, but I will be forever grateful for the kindness and compassion she offered me that day. She was another of the many angels who touched my life during this most difficult time.

About an hour after I had settled back in my room, my children came to see me. By that time, I had stopped crying, but my red, puffy eyes revealed the tears that had been shed. My children asked me what was wrong, and I told them about my emotional breakdown in the cooking class. I told them that their mother had gone from last night's "wheelchair comedian" to today's "cooking class crier." We all got a little chuckle out of that. I still smile when I think of that impromptu expression.

Jillian was true to her word. The following Monday, the mentor, whose name was Allyn, visited me in my hospital room. I could not believe what I saw. She had full mobility and complete use of all limbs on both sides of her body. She walked and talked without any evidence of impairment. Allyn told me her story and showed me a few pictures of how she had looked three-and-a-half years earlier as she lay in a hospital bed with staples and bandages on and around her head, unable to move any extremities on her left side. She explained the ups and downs she experienced during the recovery process and stressed to me the importance of the rehabilitation therapy I would receive over the next several weeks or months. Allyn encouraged me to work hard and remain focused and determined. She provided me with the hope that by doing so, perhaps I could regain the use of the left side of my body. She also told me that she was back to running, which of course provided me with even more optimism and motivation. I remember thinking how awesome it would be if one day I could be well enough to pay it forward and volunteer as a mentor. And what a bonus it would be if, like Allyn, I could regain the ability to run.

I believe it was on the same day as Allyn's visit that grooming was the subject of my occupational therapy session. The focus would be on showering and dressing. By this time, nine days since the stroke, I had become acutely aware of how difficult seemingly simple tasks of daily living could be. I was labeled a "max assist," which meant that I needed complete assistance to do anything that involved mobility of any kind. I required help getting in and out of bed, getting in and out of the wheelchair, and getting to and from the bathroom. Whenever I was being removed from the bed, a hospital belt was wrapped around my waist, providing an additional measure of security for me and the person offering assistance. The belt enabled the person to hold me up and guide me safely.

For the next two-and-a-half weeks, my occupational therapists worked with me on routine tasks of daily living such as showering, dressing, and brushing my teeth and hair. I could not believe how difficult it was to relearn these simple, basic, daily tasks.

While my occupational therapists worked with me on grooming and dressing, it was the physical therapists who focused on helping me regain the ability to stand and walk again. My primary physical therapist, Stefanie, spent hours teaching me how to safely stand up and sit down, whether it be from or to the wheelchair, bed, toilet, bench, or mat. I learned a special technique for accomplishing such simple acts as standing up or sitting down when only one side of your body is working. Stefanie also taught me how to use a cane and a walker. She also continuously kicked the back of my left foot to get it to move forward.

I remember the sadness I felt during my first few sessions in the therapy room as other patients and therapists watched Stefanie kick my flaccid leg attempting to guide me forward. I felt so helpless. I was an invalid for the first time in my life. I also recall the joy I felt and the big smile I had on my face when, in a later session, I took a few steps without any prodding. Patients and therapists in that same therapy room cheered and clapped as I moved toward them. At the time, these small improvements were considered monumental accomplishments.

In addition to occupational and physical therapy, speech and recreational therapy were also important parts of my rehabilitation program. Speech therapy consisted of one-on-one time with the therapist as well as time in group settings, where we played games such as bingo and Bananagrams. We were also shown effective and safe ways to handle some of the simple tasks of daily living, such as sorting out medications, taking money out of an ATM, and shopping and paying for groceries. The individual time as well as the group time was designed to test and improve our language, math, reasoning, and memory skills.

Recreational therapy was conducted in groups. There was, of course, the infamous first of three cooking classes that I attended during my three-week stay. I am pleased to say that no tears were shed at cooking class two or three. There were also art and music classes, where we painted, colored, and played musical jeopardy. Kristie and Hady, the recreational therapy student training under her, ran the classes with a great deal of enthusiasm and patience. They were always offering help and words of encouragement. And then there was the music therapist, Trenton, whose bright smile and joyous laughter lit up the room as he played his guitar and requested that we sing along with him. It was a special treat when Trenton was accompanied to class by the hospital therapy dog, a beautiful golden retriever named Mesa.

Three weeks and one day after my admission to the rehabilitation center, and one day shy of four weeks since my stroke, I was discharged from Memorial South inpatient care. I was scheduled to come back the following week to begin outpatient therapy. By the time of my discharge, I had regained mobility in my left foot and leg, but my walking was still quite impaired. I had to drag the left foot and sometimes needed a little kick from someone to get it started or keep it moving. I did not have confidence in my ability to walk any distance and was even uncertain if I could get out of bed and to the bathroom on my own.

In the meantime, my family and I happened to be preregistered for the two-mile scleroderma fundraising walk scheduled for the following day. It had been eight years since my scleroderma diagnosis, and my family had been participating in this annual event for the past few years. I had mentioned to Stefanie during one of my physical therapy sessions how proud I was to participate in this awareness-raising event. On the day of my discharge, my husband, Kevin, and I told Stefanie our plan: Kevin and our children would push me in the wheelchair along the two-mile route. To our surprise, Stefanie responded that she did not think they had to push me. She thought I could get out of the wheelchair and walk at least a portion of the two miles. I was completely taken aback by her response. I had not even considered that to be a possibility. In my mind, I was not yet ready for such a challenge. Nevertheless, with Stefanie's words, a seed was planted.

The following morning, we arrived at the event with the original plan intact. I remained in the wheelchair for the first half of the walk. At the midway point, however, Kevin and my daughter, Jennifer, asked me if I wanted to get out of the wheelchair and try walking part of the way. My first inclination was to say no; I still did not think I was quite ready. After some prodding from my family and a few friends who were walking with us, I was reminded of Stefanie's words from the previous day and decided I needed to at least attempt to get out of the wheelchair and walk. And with Kevin's help, I slid out of the wheelchair, and with him holding on to the safety belt wrapped securely around my waist, I stood and took one step forward. Then another step and another step. Before I knew it, I was crossing the finish line as strangers clapped and cheered. What these strangers did not know was that my impaired gait and my inability to straighten my left arm or open my clenched hand were not caused by the scleroderma. Rather, my current physical impairments were the lingering effects of the stroke, which had unexpectedly disrupted my life a mere four weeks before. As I dragged my left leg over that finish line with Kevin still holding on to my safety belt with one hand and lifting my unimpaired right arm over my head with his other hand, I was exuberant over the realization that I had walked a mile. The seed Stefanie planted had come to fruition!

My participation in the scleroderma event, walking across the finish line instead of being wheeled over it, provided me with a renewed sense of confidence. For the next several days, I navigated my way around the house more frequently and comfortably. By the time I started outpatient therapy on Tuesday, my left leg had gotten stronger, and my gait was less impaired. There was clearly a noticeable difference in the movement of the woman who had been discharged from inpatient care the preceding Thursday and the one who, five days later, was reentering the facility to begin outpatient therapy.

Throughout that first week post-discharge, the mobility of my left foot and leg continued to make remarkable improvement, which enabled me to feel more confident about my plans to participate in the Tour de Broward event scheduled for Sunday. It would be my first time partaking in this annual fundraiser, whose purpose is to support Joe DiMaggio Children's Hospital, which is part of the Memorial Healthcare System. As with the scleroderma event the previous weekend, I was planning to participate in the two-mile walk. But unlike the week before, I planned to walk across the starting line and bring the wheelchair along as a safety net in case I could not handle walking the entire distance.

But when Kevin and I arrived at the park where the event was being held, we decided to leave the wheelchair in the car as it seemed that it would be difficult to maneuver it from the parking lot through the grass and sand to where the walk was set to begin. Kevin said he would come back and get the wheelchair if at any point I felt I needed it. Much to the surprise of both of us, he did not have to return to the car to retrieve the wheelchair. I managed to walk the full two miles and was able to step across both the starting and finishing lines. The hospital belt remained clipped around my waist throughout the entire walk, but this time, it remained untouched; my husband did not need to hold on to it. He was able to walk by my side and hold my hand instead.

Participation in the Tour de Broward event added to the overall sense of confidence and optimism I was feeling about my poststroke recovery as I began my second week of outpatient therapy. While there had been remarkable improvement in the mobility of my left leg during that first week post-discharge, there had been only a minimal change when it came to the impairment of my left arm and hand. That was about to change as week 2 unfolded.

During my second week of outpatient therapy, I started to regain the ability to straighten my left arm, open my hand, and extend my fingers. This made it possible for me to begin dressing myself. I was not only able to put my clothes and shoes on without the assistance of another person or a device, I could even tie my shoelaces. This was truly an amazing accomplishment!

With the great strides that had been made in the first two weeks since my inpatient discharge, by week 3, I had gained more independence and was able to resume many of the other simple tasks of everyday living, such as cooking and cleaning. I was even able to shower by myself, standing up the entire time. Exactly three weeks after I had been discharged, my outpatient physical therapist, Jeannette, accompanied me on a light jog around the fourth floor of the facility. It was, of course, a very short distance at a slow pace inside the air-conditioned building, but it felt so good. I was grinning from ear to ear, as were Jeannette and other therapists and hospital staff we passed along the way. Some who knew me were as amazed by my improvement as I was, and many who did not know me at all nevertheless understood the magnitude of the moment.

My mobility and overall physical condition continued to improve. Two months after the stroke, I was discharged from outpatient occupational therapy, and fewer than three months poststroke, I attended my last physical therapy session.

On April 19, exactly three months after being transported by ambulance and carted into the emergency room on a stretcher, I participated in a driving evaluation course offered by the

Memorial System and was granted clearance to resume driving. The restoration of my driving privileges provided me with the opportunity to participate independently in another seemingly simple task of daily life. I was feeling hopeful about my future and the possibility of returning to a full, active, and independent lifestyle.

The professionals who dealt with similar situations daily felt that I was making a remarkable and speedy recovery. They would tell me how proud they were of me and how my hard work, determination, and perseverance had led me to this point. Many friends and family members would also say things like, "I knew you could do this." "I knew that you would regain your physical abilities as you are such a strong and determined woman and were in such good shape to begin with." I would almost always respond by saying what I knew and believed at my core to be true: "It was all due to God's grace." In my heart, I knew that had the bleed occurred in a different area of my brain, or had the bleeding not stopped when it did, I might have not survived the stroke. Or even had I survived, no matter how determined I was or how hard I worked to recover, it may have been physically impossible to regain my prestroke abilities. I believed then, and I believe now, nearly eight months poststroke, that my recovery was a blessing only made possible through the amazing grace of God.

While I am so grateful for the strides that were made during those first few weeks and months after discharge, my recovery has not been without additional challenges. There have certainly been both good and bad days, which serve to remind me that in life, we sometimes take two steps forward and one step backward.

Aftershock

One of the most significant examples of backward movement occurred nearly five months after the stroke. I suffered a seizure episode and was rushed via ambulance to the emergency room at Memorial Regional Hospital, where they once again conducted a CT scan of my brain. The scan confirmed that I had not suffered another stroke. It also showed that quite a bit of the blood from the initial stroke had dissipated.

The emergency room neurologist on staff that day happened to be the same doctor who attended to me the morning of my stroke. The same who poked his head into the machine asking me about prior seizures. This time, I was telling him, as I had told the paramedics who rushed to my home and transported me to the hospital, that I believed I had, in fact, had a seizure. Another neurologist I had been seeing poststroke mentioned to me during one of my office visits that seizures are one of the potential repercussions for patients who suffered a hemorrhagic stroke, which I had. It was generally caused by the scarring left on the brain as it healed. Based on the symptoms I experienced that morning I was certain I had suffered a seizure.

The neurologist at the emergency room, as well as the paramedics, explained that based on my description of what happened, they did not think it was a seizure. They based this on the fact that I had retained consciousness during the entire episode, was able to describe the event with such clarity, and my current thought processes were clear and coherent. In addition, the neurologist ordered an EEG, which did not show evidence of a seizure. What I later learned was that it is very common for an EEG taken several hours after a seizure not to show evidence of seizure activity having occurred. I also later learned there are certain types of seizures in which a person can remain fully conscious during the entire episode and then recall the event with clarity.

Erring on the cautious side, the attending neurologist prescribed an anti-seizure medication and directed me to spend the night in the hospital so that I could be properly monitored. I was sent home the following morning with instructions to continue taking the anti-seizure medication and avoid driving for the next six months. As instructed, I remained on the prescribed medication and refrained from driving for the following six months.

During those six months, it was recommended that a second angiogram be performed. The first one had been done in January, within the first two days of my stroke. Since the stroke had occurred nearly nine months prior and subsequent MRI tests and CT scans showed that much of the blood on the brain had dissipated, the physician would be able to see clearly whether I had an aneurysm or arteriovenous malformation (AVM). Either of these would be regarded as having caused the initial stroke and make me more susceptible to future strokes. Fortunately, the angiogram showed no evidence of either an aneurysm or AVM, and I was cleared to resume my normal physical activities. I still refrained from driving because I had not yet cleared the six-month threshold, but I did resume my very favorite activity, running.

Over the next several weeks, I enjoyed jogging along my favorite neighborhood route as well as some runs at a local park. At first, my husband would walk or ride his bicycle alongside me, but after a few weeks, I had built up enough confidence to return to running solo. I was so grateful that I had regained the physical ability to return to this activity that had provided me with so much joy and solace for the past four decades. I even reached a point where I was running at my prestroke levels.

I had no further seizure episodes during that period. At that point, I was instructed to begin weaning off the anti-seizure medicine; I was told to cut my dosage in half. I was also told that I could resume driving. This was good news. According to the doctor's instructions, I began taking the reduced dosage.

Unfortunately, the good news did not last very long. On Christmas morning 2019, three and a half weeks after starting the reduction protocol, I suffered another seizure. This time I was on a run, and this time, the episode shook me to my core. Fortunately, because it was Christmas, Kevin was home and had decided to accompany me. He was riding his bicycle next to me when I suddenly told him I had to stop running because I did not feel right. I was experiencing the same type of strange sensation I had felt in that seizure-like episode six months prior. I asked Kevin to please not let me fall and to lay me down on the grass. I began having convulsions. Kevin called 911, and once again, I was transported via ambulance to Hollywood Memorial Hospital. Once again, I remained fully conscious during the entire episode and was able to respond coherently to the paramedic's and the doctor's questions. This time, however, the doctors agreed that this was a seizure. They put me back on the full dose of the anti-seizure medication and advised me that I would need to remain on anti-seizure medicine for the rest of my life.

I stated earlier that this seizure event shook me to my core. I began suffering from quite a bit of anxiety and depression, and I found myself so fearful of having another seizure. For the next several months, I sought advice from a couple of seizure specialists. At one point, it was thought that the anti-seizure medication I was taking was the primary cause of my fear and anxiety. So I was switched to a different medication. Unfortunately, the new medication did not control my seizure activity, even after the prescribed dosage was increased several times. So after several months, I was weaned off the newer medication and placed back on the original anti-seizure drug.

It has now been three and a half years since that Christmas Day episode. I have to admit that it has been a very challenging few years. Feelings of anxiety and depression have for the first time become staples in my life. As we know, life, by its very nature, is unpredictable. But having a seizure disorder—epilepsy—presents an entirely new and direct realm of unpredictability. But with medication, psychotherapy, and healthy lifestyle choices, such as adequate sleep, good nutrition, exercise, and limiting stress, I feel I can maintain some control over this frightening condition. Yet the fear of having a seizure is always percolating underneath the surface of my everyday activities. Not a day goes by that the thought of the possibility of having a seizure does not cross my mind. This condition has impacted my everyday life far more than my battle with scleroderma or the short-term disability I experienced after the hemorrhagic stroke. While I am back to driving, I have for the most part given up my daily runs. I now do the elliptical or treadmill. I occasionally go on a limited walk or run, but if I do, I no longer feel comfortable doing it solo.

Living with epilepsy has altered my feeling of independence. It has forced me to accept new limitations in how I go about my everyday life. It has required me to dig deep and to remind myself of all the valuable lessons learned thus far on my journey: to be grateful for all of the wonderful aspects of my life, my loved ones, family, and friends; to accept the circumstances that have made their way into this stage of my life; to have faith that all is as it is meant to be; to trust that God's grace will continue to guide and protect me as I continue moving forward; to remember the Serenity Prayer of accepting the things I cannot change, having the courage to change the things I can, and being blessed with the wisdom to know the difference.

Epilogue: Must History Repeat Itself?

I find it fascinating that as much as the world around me has changed over the past several decades, in many ways, social issues seem as though much has remained the same.

I look back on the marches that were at the forefront of the turbulent 1960s, when people rose to protest an unpopular war and to demand voting rights and civil rights for all. I realize the issues that sparked those marches are not very different from those fueling the civil unrest we witness today. War, racism, bigotry, and the seeds of hate, violence, and intolerance that grow from them are still too prevalent. Cries for peace, equality, and justice continue to be chanted, but too often, they seem to go unheard. Indeed, the twenty-first century is plagued by many of the same problems and much of the same adversity that defined the previous century. This realization causes me to pause and ask: How is this possible? What does it say about who we are as a species? Have we not learned from past mistakes? Are we evolving at all?

As I ponder these questions, delving deep in search of answers, I am reminded of two well-known quotations. The first is attributed to the French writer Jean-Baptiste Alphonse Karr: "The more things change, the more they stay the same."

The second is that of the American writer Hugh Prather: "Just when I think I have learned the way to live, life changes." What also comes to my mind is a quote I saw many years ago. The source I do not recall, but the message I do remember. To the best of my recollection, it states, "Just when you think you have arrived, life changes, and you are left the same as when you began."

The similar message contained in each of these statements resonates with me and leads me to wonder whether this is perhaps the essence of it all. Could it be that our life journeys are meant to be continual cycles of ups and downs, ebbs and flows, periods to reap and times to sow? Could it be that just when we think we have found our way, we suddenly find ourselves feeling lost once again? It is as though we are constantly taking two steps backward for every one step forward.

I believe it is our mission to accept these patterns and to recognize that we must surrender to forces beyond our control while continuing to persevere with quiet determination. We cannot allow ourselves to give in to the negativity we encounter or give up when we reach obstacles along the way. We must not be discouraged by the forces of resistance that attempt to push us back. We must not compromise our values. We must remember to listen to our inner voice and stay true to our heart's calls. Most important, I believe in what Mahatma Gandhi wisely advised: "You must be the change you wish to see in the world." If we want a compassionate, kind, loving, and peaceful world, then we as living, breathing beings must show compassion, kindness, and love toward one another. We must also be willing to stand up and speak out against forces that threaten equality and justice, and that violate human rights and the very essence of our humanity. We must continue to seek light from the darkness. And perhaps in the process, we will find that we have indeed grown firmer, simpler, quieter, warmer. I trust that my journey will continue to lead me in that direction.

Printed in the United States
by Baker & Taylor Publisher Services